Praise for *Th*

"Carter has produced the r argued treatise I have ever read...To be recommended for everyone who has ever inquired about the real nature of his or her own consciousness. Reading this book will be a mind-blowing clarification."

—**ERVIN LASZLO**, author of *Science and the Akashic Field*

"Carter argues that, based on the scientific research on mediumship, after-death communication, near-death experiences, end-of life experiences, terminal lucidity, apparitions, and spontaneous memories of previous lives at an early age, there is overwhelming evidence that there is a continuity of consciousness after the death of our body."

—**PIM VAN LOMMEL**, cardiologist, NDE researcher, and author of *Consciousness Beyond Life*

"A stunning contribution. Carter aptly addresses the important question of what happens after death."

—**ROBERT ALMEDER**, Professor Emeritus of Philosophy, Georgia State, and author of *Death & Personal Survival: The Evidence for Life after Death*

"What makes this book different from anything else in the literature is its wider coverage of the various types of evidence, and its robust demolition of the hypotheses used by opponents to debunk the evidence...Carter writes with the flair of a novelist rather than a stodgy social scientist."

—**STAFFORD BETTY**, Professor Emeritus of Religious Studies, California State University, Bakersfield, and author of *The Afterlife Unveiled*

"Both original and convincing. It is original because Carter provides his readers with a tool kit that they can use to evaluate the evidence as well as the alternatives. It is convincing because Carter presents data from diverse sources…He engages his readers, ultimately allowing them to draw their own conclusions."

—**STANLEY KRIPPNER, PhD**, Affiliated Distinguished Professor, California Institute of Integral Studies

"Carter lays out some of the best evidence derived from a variety of sources…while demonstrating unequivocally that non-paranormal explanations fail to cover the facts…This book is essential reading for those on both sides of this controversy."

—**MICHAEL PRESCOTT**, author of *The Far Horizon*

"Carter offers some of the very best evidence available to us…Evidence that both mainstream science and orthodox religions have failed to grasp or appreciate. Carter presents it in a logical, cogent, and compelling manner."

—**MICHAEL TYMN**, author of *The Afterlife Revealed*

"A significant and penetrating contribution…It combines rigorous logic with extensive case histories…On the basis of multiple lines of evidence, Carter makes a compelling and entirely reasonable *Case for the Afterlife.*"

—**DAVID LORIMER**, author of *Survival? Death as a Transition*

"A comprehensive examination of all the phenomena that would suggest persistence of some characteristics of personhood after the body is gone."

—**ROBERT BOBROW, MD**, author of *The Witch in the Waiting Room*

The Case for the
Afterlife

© Chris Carter

About the Author

Chris Carter was educated at Oxford and is the author of three highly acclaimed books and several published articles dealing with controversial issues at the intersection of science and philosophy. After working in the field of finance, Carter currently devotes his time to writing, playing racquet sports, and teaching physics.

The Case for the

Afterlife

Evidence of Life **AFTER DEATH**

CHRIS CARTER

WOODBURY, MINNESOTA

FIRST EDITION
First Printing, 2025

Book design by Rordan Brasington
Cover design by Kevin R. Brown
Interior illustrations by Llewellyn Art Department

Llewellyn Publications is a registered trademark of Llewellyn Worldwide Ltd.

Library of Congress Cataloging-in-Publication Data (Pending)
ISBN: 978-0-7387-7956-0

Llewellyn Worldwide Ltd. does not participate in, endorse, or have any authority or responsibility concerning private business transactions between our authors and the public.

All mail addressed to the author is forwarded but the publisher cannot, unless specifically instructed by the author, give out an address or phone number.

Any internet references contained in this work are current at publication time, but the publisher cannot guarantee that a specific location will continue to be maintained. Please refer to the publisher's website for links to authors' websites and other sources.

Llewellyn Publications
A Division of Llewellyn Worldwide Ltd.
2143 Wooddale Drive
Woodbury, MN 55125-2989
www.llewellyn.com

Printed in the United States of America

Other Books by Chris Carter

Science and Psychic Phenomena: The Fall of the House of Skeptics
(former edition titled *Parapsychology & the Skeptics*)

Science and the Near-Death Experience

Science and the Afterlife

Debating Psychic Experience (contributing author, edited by Stan
Krippner and Harris Friedman)

Forthcoming Books by Chris Carter

The Case Against Standardized Tests

I regard the existence of discarnate spirits as scientifically proved and I no longer refer to the skeptic as having any right to speak on the subject. Any man who does not accept the existence of discarnate spirits and the proof of it is either ignorant or a moral coward. I give him short shrift, and do not propose any longer to argue with him on the supposition that he knows anything about the subject.

—James H. Hyslop, professor of logic and ethics, General Secretary of the American Society for Psychical Research 1905–1920

Contents

Prologue

His name was Barry, and he was a fellow student at our college residence at Oxford. That evening, Barry was trying to convince me to join him and two other graduate students to spend our next year living in a large and ancient farmhouse owned by our college, which lay on picturesque farmland just outside of town. As an expatriate student from Canada, I was not sure if I wanted to leave the residence, which was much closer to town and college. But Barry was relentless:

"The place has a ghost."

His words caught my attention. I had heard of England being described as "the Haunted Isle," but had never given the matter any serious thought.

"Has anyone seen anything?"

"No," he replied, "but there have been a lot of strange sounds reported."

I decided to visit the farm to see the place for myself, which turned out to be a two-story stone house. While there, I stopped to speak with the college carpenter, who had his workshop on the property. After a brief chat, I came straight out with it:

"I hear the place is haunted."

"Well, I don't know myself," he said, "but the carpenter before me, he *swore* the place was haunted."

That was enough for me. I decided to accept my friends' offer and join them, to spend the next year living in the old farmhouse.

To make a long story short, over the next year I did indeed see and hear some unusual things, which I could not readily explain. Hauntings and the like did not fit in with the materialist opinions of some of the philosophers I had studied. And yet, I was open-minded enough to admit the possibility that perhaps these experiences were of just what they seemed to be: the lingering, disembodied presence of someone who had lived in the house in days long past.

After graduation, I returned to Canada and began to reflect on my strange experiences in the old farmhouse. These had not been very dramatic, consisting of little more than doors occasionally slamming for no apparent reason, a wall decoration mysteriously moving in front of my eyes, and the fleeting sound of a woman's voice, seemingly out of thin air. I did not think for one moment that these odd experiences proved anything, but they did arouse my interest. It seemed to me that other folks must have reported similar experiences, and so I wondered if any serious research had been done on such matters as hauntings and seeming communication with the deceased. During a visit to the local library, I was surprised to find several books dealing with these and other related topics. I began to read.

I soon discovered that plenty of people throughout history and around the world had indeed reported similar experiences to my own, and often of a *much* more dramatic and evidential nature. I was astonished by the quantity and quality of research completed over the previous century. Particularly impressive was the enormous volume of evidence so carefully gathered by the British and American Societies for Psychical Research, both founded in the 1880s, whose members included some of the era's most highly regarded scientists, philosophers, lawyers, and scholars, on both sides of the Atlantic.

All of this came as a shocking revelation. As I read more deeply over the next several years, I became increasingly convinced by the evidence that we survive the deaths of our bodies. Some of the lines of evidence, such as the near-death experience, seemed to indicate not only that we survive, but also that dying is a beautiful experience, and that the afterlife is in a vast world of almost unimaginable loveliness.

However, I was also aware of the famous saying by the physicist Richard Feynman: "You must not fool yourself, and you are the easiest person to fool." I began to wonder if I were suffering from what is known as the confirmation bias: the tendency of most of us to seek out sources of information that confirm what we already believe, and to avoid information that conflicts with our opinions. The only way for us to avoid this confirmation bias is to seek out material that challenges our ideas, and to listen to dissenting views. And so, wondering if I were indeed fooling myself, I began to seek out any dissenting views that I could find.

With little effort, I discovered a website devoted solely to debunking belief in the afterlife. I was shocked by the vehemence of the author, and by his sheer ignorance of the best evidence. The quotes he supplied from other so-called skeptics were equally unimpressive. I wrote to the author via email to state my objections, and he replied. Over the next few weeks we engaged in an online debate, and I gained great insight into the "skeptical" way of thinking about these issues.

I decided a book was needed to critically examine these arguments, and the result was my first book, *Parapsychology and the Skeptics* (later renamed by my second publisher to *Science and Psychic Phenomena: The Fall of the House of Skeptics*). This was followed by two more books: the second examining the near-death experience, and the third exploring three other compelling lines of evidence for survival. At the end of all this research and writing—after years of examining both the evidence for and the skeptical arguments against—I emerged even *more* confident that the evidence for survival was convincing beyond all reasonable doubt.

It is important to remember that most of the so-called skeptics are militant atheists. One of the fundamental pillars of the atheistic worldview is the doctrine of materialism: the ancient idea that all events ultimately have a material cause, and therefore, that the mind is produced by the physical workings of the brain. It follows from this that the mind cannot exist in the absence of a functioning brain. Any evidence to the contrary provides a direct challenge to materialism, and thus threatens the collapse of this entire worldview.

When faced with evidence that contradicts our preconceived ideas, we may enter into an uncomfortable state of tension the psychologists call *cognitive dissonance*. In this situation we have a choice: give the contradictory evidence serious consideration, or simply dismiss it. The first option requires time and effort and brings with it the risk that we may be forced to change our opinions. Since we tend to hold on to our opinions as prized possessions, simply dismissing the objectional evidence is always the easier option.

True skepticism involves the *suspension* of belief, not the *refusal* of belief, and so most of the so-called skeptics are not skeptics at all, but simply deniers.

While debating atheists and other so-called skeptics, a common retort I hear is, "Well, you just *want* to believe it's true." I simply reply: "And I guess you *don't* want it to be true. Perhaps you don't want to be held accountable for your life. And anyway, instead of criticizing me as a person, why don't you try criticizing my arguments? *Or is that just too hard?*"

It should be obvious that the motivation behind such an accusation is the desire to stop thinking on the subject, rather than stimulate it. And—quite apart from the sheer laziness of the desperate accusation *you just want to believe it*—it should also be obvious that *nothing* follows from it. If a man wants to believe his wife is faithful, that does not mean she is unfaithful.

True skepticism is a double-edged sword that can be applied to any claim, including the claims of the skeptics. The philosopher Curt Ducasse made this point forcefully:

> Although the evidence offered by addicts of the marvelous for the reality of the phenomena they accept must be critically examined, it is equally necessary on the other side to scrutinize just as closely and critically the skeptic's allegations of fraud, or of mal-observation, or of misinterpretation of what was observed, or of hypnotically induced hallucinations. *For there is likely to be just as much wishful thinking, prejudice, emotion, snap judgment, naïveté, and intellectual dishonesty on the side of orthodoxy, of skepticism, and of conservatism, as on the side of hunger for and belief in the marvelous.*[1]

Christianity and the Evidence for Survival Are Compatible

The evidence in favor of survival is vast and varied and comes from five independent lines of evidence. Committed Christians

---

1. Ducasse, *Paranormal Science and Life After Death*, 35. Emphasis in original.

may have trouble with some of these lines, but I hope to show that there are good reasons to believe that these lines of evidence are not incompatible with Christianity. Indeed, it can be argued that they are supported by both scripture and theology.

Consider one line of evidence discussed in detail here: communication with the deceased via human mediums. Based upon certain passages from the Old Testament, some Christians believe that such communication should neither be attempted nor taken seriously. Yet several passages from the New Testament do not seem to prohibit such communion, although they urge caution:

"Beloved, believe not every spirit, but test the spirits to see whether they are of God."[2]

If we think there is no reason to suppose that the change called death suddenly transforms bad people into good, then of course it is wise to "test the spirits."

In this next passage Jesus is referring to false prophets, but it also seems relevant here:

"By their fruits you shall know them."[3]

Commenting on this very passage, author Miles Edward Allen wrote:

If the results of a spirit communication are alleviation of grief, enhanced compassion, reduction of anxiety, a feeling of being closer to God, and other such positive feelings and actions, then what role could the devil be playing? What sort of demon goes around encouraging folks to love one another?[4]

Author Michael Tymn agrees:

---

2. 1 John 4:1.

3. Matthew 7:20.

4. Allen, *The Realities of Heaven*, 44–45.

I try to explain to my orthodox Christian friends that most of the mediumistic messages are benevolent in one way or another, urging love, compassion, kindness, and empathy, and that psychical research supports the basic tenet of their faith, that consciousness survives death in a larger life. Moreover, many of them pay homage to Jesus, but the usual reaction is that the "spirits" are simply "wolves in sheep's clothing" trying to lure people into Satan's camp before pulling the rug out from under them. I agree that one has to be on guard for low-level spirits; that's why we are told in Scripture "to test the spirits, whether they are of God," and to discern the messages.[5]

The earliest writings in the New Testament are thought to be the letters of Paul. In *First Corinthians*, he claims, "In each of us the Spirit is manifested in one particular way, for some useful purpose. One man, through the gift of Spirit has gifts of healing, and another miraculous powers: another has the gift of prophecy, and another the ability to distinguish true spirits from false."[6]

Other writings seem to indicate that the early Christians did indeed spend time communing with spirits. For instance, the early Christian writer Tertullian (160–220 CE) described a woman whose gifts include "revelation, which she experiences in the Spirit by ecstatic vision amidst the sacred rites of the Lord's Day in the church. She converses with angels, and sometimes even with the Lord; she both sees and hears mysterious communications."[7] (The reader may be interested to note that Tertullian also argued that apparitions and what are today called near-death experiences are evidence for survival, in addition to biblical writing.) It was only after politicians and an entrenched priesthood commandeered the

---

5. Tymn, "Bible Scholar Explores Modern Psychic Phenomena."

6. 1 Corinthians 12:8–10.

7. As quoted in Potts and Devanno, "Tertullian's Theory of the Soul," 213.

church in the third century that the right of men and women to commune with the deceased was revoked.

Several modern theologians agree that the evidence supplements their faith. The Reverend Charles Drayton Thomas, whom we will meet again later in this book, was a Methodist minister who for many years was an active member of the British Society of Psychical Research and participated in many sittings with renowned mediums. He wrote:

> Perhaps it will be asked what benefit may be expected from a general acceptance of this evidence for survival. I think it will do for others what it has done for me. It has supplemented and reinforced my faith, both in times of bereavement and in the prospect of old age and death. Also, it has further emphasized the value of personal religion.[8]

Father Pere Francois Brune, a Catholic priest and theologian, has written about how the Catholic Church's attitude about communication from the afterlife is changing:

> We do not have an official change in the Church's position. But it is in fact an evolution that without any doubt is due to the realization that the phenomena exist, and that they indeed correspond very often to an authentic communication with our dead.[9]

A Church of England committee thoroughly studied records of mediumship for two years, analyzing data and sitting with some of the leading mediums in England at the time. At the end of the investigation, seven of the ten members were outspoken with this

---

8. Quoted in Horgan, *Your Eternal Self*, 101.

9. Quoted in Horgan, *Your Eternal Self*, 101. See also Brune, *The Undiscovered Beyond*.

conclusion: "The hypothesis that they [spirit communications] proceed in some cases from discarnate spirits is the true one."[10]

Perhaps the line of evidence for survival most troubling to modern Christians is the idea of reincarnation. However, we will see that several theologians and philosophers have argued that there is nothing incompatible about reincarnation with the teachings of Jesus of Nazareth. For instance, philosopher Robert Almeder has dealt with this issue at length, and has concluded that "there are sound scriptural, traditional, and philosophical reasons for Christians to endorse the belief in reincarnation" and that "there is nothing inconsistent with believing in the core doctrines of Christianity and simultaneously believing in some form of reincarnation."[11] For instance, reincarnation helps answer the age-old question of how we can reconcile a belief in the goodness of God with all of the undeserved suffering and undeserved good fortune we so often encounter in this world. Theologian Geddes MacGregor wrote:

> Reincarnation takes care of the problem of moral injustice. To the age-old question of Job (why do the wicked prosper and the righteous suffer?) the reincarnationist has a ready answer: we are seeing, in this life, only a fragment of a long story. Death is but the end of a chapter, it is not the end of the story.[12]

And, as Leslie Weatherhead, former president of the British Methodist Conference, asked in his "The Case for Reincarnation" lecture, "If I failed to pass those examinations in life which can only be taken while I dwell in a physical body, shall I not have to come back and take them again?"[13]

---

10. Horgan, *Your Eternal Self*, 102.

11. Almeder, *Death & Personal Survival*, 81.

12. Almeder, *Death & Personal Survival*, 75.

13. Almeder, *Death & Personal Survival*, 76.

In southern Europe at least some Christians believed in reincarnation, and church leaders tolerated the belief as acceptable until the Second Council of Constantinople in 553 AD. It has been pointed out by several theologians that the actions of this council did not constitute an official ban, as the council was not called by the Pope, who refused to attend. Rather, it was called by the Byzantine Emperor Justinian, and it seems that the condemnations were politically motivated, being what Justinian thought he needed to maintain harmony.[14]

In recent years there has been a growing number of Christian theologians calling for a serious reconsideration of reincarnation, one example being Geddes MacGregor. In his book *Reincarnation in Christianity,* he mentions the following from the gospel of John concerning a man born blind whom Jesus cured:

> As Jesus passed by, he saw a man blind from birth. And his disciples asked him, "Rabbi, who has sinned, this man or his parents, that he was born blind?"[15]

This would indicate that the disciples accepted the idea of reincarnation, and Jesus did not rebuke them in his reply.

In the gospel of Matthew the disciples ask Jesus how he can be the Messiah when Elijah has not yet returned. They are referring to the Old Testament prophecy of Malachi that God will send Elijah back before the arrival of the Messiah. In his reply Jesus asserts that Elijah has returned in the person of John the Baptist:

> As they went away, Jesus began to speak to the crowd concerning John … "This is he of whom it is written, 'Behold I send my messenger before you, who shall prepare your way before

---

14. For an extended discussion of Christianity and reincarnation, see Almeder, *Death and Personal Survival*, 64–81.

15. John 9:1–2.

you.' Truly I say to you, among those born of woman there has arisen no one greater than John the Baptist … And if you are willing to accept it, he is Elijah who was to come.[16]

And for those who may find the idea of endless reincarnation an unpleasant prospect, we will see later that such fears are unfounded. There are reasons to believe that most of us only incarnate two, three, or at most four times. Once the lessons of earth-life are learned, there is simply no reason to repeat them.

• • •

The purpose of this book is to consider the strongest evidence for survival from several independent lines of evidence and to carefully evaluate the skeptical objections. The supreme irony of all the counterarguments to the reality of survival is this: if a person has a solid grasp of the best evidence, then a critical examination of these counterarguments results in an even *greater* conviction that the case for the afterlife has been established beyond all reasonable doubt.

I have never been much troubled by the abstract fear that my time on Earth is finite. And yet, many of us are haunted by the lingering fear of death, like a vulture circling constantly over our heads. Whether you feel this anxiety, or are merely curious about this ancient mystery, this book is for you.

---

16. Matthew 11:11–15.

Introduction

The belief in an afterlife dates back at least to the Neanderthals, who buried their dead with flowers, jewelry, and utensils, presumably for use in the next world. And throughout recorded history people have reported many phenomena that would seem to indicate evidence of survival past the point of bodily death. Could the nearly universal nature of cultural belief in some sort of survival be based upon experiences humans have reported in all known cultures for thousands of years?

The evidence in favor of an afterlife is vast, varied, and ancient: it comes from near-death experiences, deathbed visions, apparitions, children who remember previous lives, and apparent communications from the departed received via human mediums. These lines of evidence, very different from each other, all point in the same direction.

These impressive lines of evidence will be examined in this book. Yet various objections have been raised against all of them. Thus, much more than "mere" evidence needs to be provided if we are to decisively settle this controversial issue; it is also necessary to carefully examine these objections to see if they withstand critical scrutiny.

As we will see, many of these objections—such as fraud or mistaken eyewitness testimony—are easily dealt with. Others are intractable, and so continue to appear in the literature decade after decade, with no apparent resolution in clear sight. The far and away most stubbornly persistent of these intractable objections is the often-cited protest that various forms of superpowerful extrasensory perception may more simply explain the evidence.

The idea that extrasensory perception (ESP) could be used to plausibly explain the evidence for survival, including apparent communication from the dead via human mediums, is an idea that persistently appears in the literature on survival, decade after decade. After the idea that mediumistic communication could be explained as simple ESP between medium and sitter was refuted by the invention of proxy sittings (in which a third party with no connection to the deceased visits the medium as a proxy sitter), the theory of *Super*-ESP was advanced: that is, the idea that mediums may unconsciously employ vast, virtually unlimited powers of telepathy and clairvoyance, far superior in scope and power than anything documented in other contexts, with the purpose of deceiving both sitters and themselves that the dead are in fact communicating.

I argue in this book that the theory of Super-ESP has no rational foundation, and that it is nothing more than an excuse to not accept the most straightforward inference from the data. I further argue here that the reason the theory of Super-ESP has stubbornly persisted as a seemingly legitimate counterexplanation to survival is due to ongoing confusion over several fundamental yet intractable issues, and to the fact that proponents of Super-ESP never explicitly deal with these issues, but simply ignore them.

These issues would include the mind-body relationship; the nature of evidence; the various standards of proof, the nature of proof beyond all reasonable doubt, and where the burden of proof should properly be placed; the difference between real and purely imaginary possibilities; and the nature of science.

This book will examine the most convincing evidence for survival, and the most convincing evidence is that which cannot be explained away by the usual suspects of fraud, mistaken eyewitness testimony, incompetence, or—as a desperate last resort—by any reference to extrasensory perception, *super or otherwise*. It is my intention to provide here, in one place, a long-awaited resolution to the controversy over survival.

However, first we need to deal with the issues underlying the most intractable objections, in order that we may then have the tools at hand necessary to deal with these objections whenever they are raised.

The remainder of this book will therefore follow this outline:

Part I: The Tool Kit. This section will provide the reader with all the tools necessary to evaluate both the evidence and the skeptical objections to this evidence. It lays the theoretical foundations for everything that follows, and these powerful tools can be applied to an astonishingly wide variety of controversial issues: not just the survival question, but everything from evaluating such matters as the guilt or innocence of an accused, the claims that an election was stolen, and even to the issue of whether or not men have walked on the moon. But first, we will start by examining the mind-body relationship, as some critics insist that survival can be ruled out from the start for *a priori* reasons. This opinion is based upon an unstated assumption, and we will see that there are plenty of good reasons to question this assumption. We then examine the nature of evidence, including the reliability of eyewitness testimony and the technique of inference to the best explanation. The various standards of proof are discussed, including the all-important standard of proof beyond reasonable doubt. We finish this section with a discussion of the nature of science and the difference between science, metaphysics, and ideology.

Part II: The Evidence. This section examines the most compelling cases supporting survival, from five independent lines of evidence. We begin with the near-death experience: millions of people worldwide have reported strange experiences that give every indication of having occurred during a time when there was every medical reason to believe they were clinically dead. Some of the most common counterexplanations are carefully examined, and found wanting. Next, we consider deathbed visions: those near death commonly experience visions of being greeted by departed friends, relatives, and religious figures. This is followed by cases of children who claim to remember previous lives, and the reader may be surprised to learn that such cases are widely reported across various cultures. Then, we examine detailed reports of apparitions: these are also widely reported across cultures, some have been seen by several people at the same time, and some seem to show a purpose only of their own. Finally, and most impressive, are messages from the dead. These too have been reported across various cultures for thousands of years, and the reader will come to understand why this is the single most evidential line of the five lines of evidence discussed.

Part III: RIP Super-ESP. The reader has now seen that extrasensory perception among the living—whether super or otherwise—is simply incapable of explaining the very best cases for survival. In this section we will consider some final points in the light of all that we have covered. We begin with asking if there is any reason to believe that *Super*-ESP—that is, virtually unlimited powers of telepathy and clairvoyance—even exists. This is followed by an examination of the arguments of philosopher Stephan Braude, the main proponent of Super-ESP as a counterexplanation to the idea of survival. Braude's arguments are critically examined, and found to be based upon serious misconceptions. Finally, we bind everything together, and using the technique of inference to the best explanation, we clearly see how the various lines of evidence converge toward an astounding conclusion.

Part I
The Tool Kit

After finishing this section, the reader will have all the tools necessary to deal with the most common skeptical objections. Chapter 1 deals with the single most fundamental materialist objection. Once this is dispatched, the next two chapters deal with how evidence should rationally be evaluated, and where the burden of proof should properly be placed. Finally, chapter 4 discusses the nature of science.

Chapter 1
The Mind-Body Relationship

The nature of the human mind is the most important question in philosophy, psychiatry, and psychology. And the nature of the relationship between mind and body is also the most central and fundamental question in the debate between those who accept and those who deny the reality of survival of the mind after the death of the body. Many "skeptics" assert that it is simply "impossible" for the mind to operate independently of a properly functioning brain. For instance, psychologist Gardner Murphy and editor Laura Dale have remarked that, regardless of the evidence, "it is the biological and the philosophical difficulty with survival that holds us back, not really the unacceptability of the evidence."[17] So, our first order of business will be to closely examine the relationship between mind and brain, in order to deal with this, the most fundamental skeptical objection to the survival of the mind after the death of the brain.

The Roman poet Lucretius wrote one of the earliest treatises advancing the arguments that the relation between

---

17. Quoted in Kelly et al., *Irreducible Mind*, 598.

mind and body is so close that the mind depends upon the body and therefore cannot exist without it. Similar arguments, to the effect that the mind is a function of the brain, were taken up with greater force centuries later, in the work of men such as Thomas Huxley, defender of Darwinism, and Corliss Lamont, former president of the American Humanist Association.

Huxley, a friend and colleague of Charles Darwin, described the mind as a mere *epiphenomenon*, that is, a useless byproduct of brain activity that has no causal effect.

Although Darwin liked and admired Huxley, he would have none of Huxley's theory of the one-sided action of body on mind. Supporting Huxley's opinion would have contradicted his life's work, as Darwin correctly realized that his theory required the mutual interaction of mind and body. For if thoughts and feelings did not lead to useful actions in the physical world, then mind would be useless. But then it could not have evolved by natural selection. So, even from a strictly Darwinian approach, the minds of animals and men should be expected to lead to useful actions, and should therefore be a causal influence in nature.

Corliss Lamont, former president of the American Humanist Association, rightly contends that the fundamental issue in any discussion of survival is the relationship of mind to body, and divides the various positions into two broad categories: monism, which asserts that mind and body are bound together and cannot exist apart; and dualism, which asserts that mind and body are separable entities that may exist apart. Lamont offers several reasons why he believes that the facts support monism: destruction of brain tissue by disease or injury can impair normal mental activity; a severe blow to the head may cause unconsciousness; and alcohol and other drugs can affect the mind. Following Lucretius,

Lamont and several other modern writers are convinced that the facts of modern science weigh heavily in favor of monism.

In summary, their various arguments against the possibility of survival are: (1) the effects of dementia, drugs, and a blow to the head on the mind; (2) the effect of brain damage on mental activity, and specifically, the fact that lesions of certain regions of the brain eliminates or impairs particular capacities; and (3) the idea that memories are stored in the brain and therefore cannot survive the destruction of the brain. The inference they all draw from these observations is that the correlation of mental and physical processes is so close that it is inconceivable how the mind could exist apart from the brain. Except for the appeals of the modern writers to the terminology of neuroscience, the arguments advanced in favor of the dependence of the mental on the physical are essentially the same as those advanced by Lucretius.

However, there are really two separate issues here: one is the *logical* possibility of survival, and the other is the *empirical* possibility. There is no self-contradiction in the assertion that consciousness may exist in the absence of a functioning brain, and so survival is at the very least a logical possibility. The question then becomes whether or not survival is an empirical possibility—that is, whether or not the idea of survival is compatible with the facts and laws of nature as currently understood.

Implicit Assumption behind the Empirical Arguments against the Possibility of Survival

It is crucial to realize that all the arguments mentioned above that are opposed to the empirical possibility of survival are based upon a certain assumption of the relationship between mind and body that usually goes unstated. For instance, one of the arguments mentioned earlier starts with the observation that a severe blow to the head can cause the cessation of consciousness; from this it is concluded that consciousness is produced by a properly functioning brain, and so cannot exist in its absence.

However, this conclusion is not based on the evidence alone. There is an implicit, unstated assumption behind this argument, and it is often unconsciously employed. The hidden premise behind this argument can be illustrated with the analogy of listening to music on a radio, smashing the radio's receiver, and thereby concluding that the radio was *producing* the music. The implicit assumption made in all the arguments discussed above was that the relationship between brain activity and consciousness was always one of cause to effect, and never that of *effect to cause*. But this assumption is not known to be true, and it is not the only conceivable one consistent with the observed facts mentioned earlier. Just as consistent with the observed facts is the idea that the brain's function is that of an intermediary between mind and body—or in other words, that the brain's function is that of a two-way receiver-transmitter—sometimes from body to mind, and sometimes from mind to body.

The idea that the brain functions as an intermediary between mind and body is an ancient one, and like the materialist theory, this ancient argument also has its modern proponents, in the form of several philosophers, psychologists, and neurologists. These would include: philosopher and psychologist William James; philosophers Curt Ducasse, Robert Almeder, and Neal Grossman; renowned neuroscientists and Nobel Laureates Wilder Penfield and Sir John Eccles; neurologists Gary Schwartz and Mario Beauregard; and the psychologist Cyril Burt. The latter elegantly summarized the transmission hypothesis:

The brain is not an organ that generates consciousness, but rather an instrument evolved to transmit and limit the processes of consciousness and of conscious attention so as to restrict them to those aspects of the material environment which at any moment are crucial for the terrestrial success of the individual.[18]

What about the statement that the production hypothesis is somehow "simpler," and for this reason should be preferred? In 1898 the American psychologist and philosopher William James delivered the Ingersoll Lecture, in which he wrote that the production of consciousness by the brain, if it does in fact occur, is "as far as our understanding goes, as great a miracle as if we said, thought is 'spontaneously generated,' or 'created out of nothing.'"

The theory of production is therefore not a jot more simple or credible in itself than any other conceivable theory. It is only a little more popular. All that one need do, therefore, if the ordinary materialist should challenge one to explain how the brain *can* be an organ for limiting and determining to a certain form a consciousness elsewhere produced, is to ask him in turn to explain how it can be an organ for producing consciousness out of whole cloth. For polemic purposes, the two theories are thus exactly on a par.

Two theoretical objections to dualism that are often raised by materialist philosophers are (1) the interaction problem, and (2) the notion that dualism contradicts the physics principle of energy conservation. We will now see that neither of these objections carries any weight whatsoever.

---

18. Cyril, *ESP and Psychology*, 60.

The Interaction of Mind and Body

Critics of dualism will often question how two very different entities such as mind and matter can possibly interact. As K. R. Rao writes,

> The main problem with such dualism is the problem of interaction. How does unextended mind interact with the extended body? Any kind of causal interaction between them, which is presumed by most dualist theories, comes into conflict with the physical theory that the universe is a closed system and that every physical event is linked with an antecedent physical event. This *assumption* preempts any possibility that a mental act can cause a physical event.[19]

There are two problems with the above. First of all, the assumption that the universe is a closed system is *not* a physical theory but rather a *metaphysical assumption* once held by some classical physicists (certainly not held by Newton and Maxwell, both deeply religious). This assumption does not follow directly from anything in classical physics. An argument has also been made by Wigner, Neumann, and others that modern physics—quantum mechanics—has brought mind back into nature and has thus eliminated the causal closure of the physical. Many modern physicists believe that that the universe is not a closed system and that the collapse of the wave function—a physical event—is linked with an antecedent mental event.[20]

Second, by asking "How does unextended mind interact with the extended body?" Rao is implicitly assuming that things can only interact with other things with which they share some common characteristic. But as David Hume pointed out long ago, we

---

19. Rao, "Consciousness." Emphasis added.
20. See Appendix I for an in-depth discussion of quantum physics.

form our ideas of causation by observation of constant correlation; since anything could in principle correlate with anything else, only observation can establish what interacts with what.

Parapsychologist John Beloff has considered the issue logically:

> If an event A never occurred without being preceded by some other event B, we would surely want to say that the second event was a necessary condition or cause of the first event, *whether or not* the two had anything else in common. As for such a principle being an empirical truth, how could it be since there are here only two known independent substances, i.e. mind and matter, as candidates on which to base a generalization? To argue that they cannot interact *because* they are independent is to beg the question … It says something about the desperation of those who want to dismiss radical dualism that such phony arguments should repeatedly be invoked by highly reputable philosophers who should know better.[21]

Would Dualism Violate Energy Conservation?

Daniel Dennett's book *Consciousness Explained* has a chapter titled "Why Dualism Is Forlorn" in which he asks, "What is so wrong with dualism?" His answer:

> A fundamental principle of physics is that any change in the trajectory of a particle is an acceleration requiring the expenditure of energy … this principle of conservation of energy … is apparently violated by dualism. This confrontation between standard physics and dualism has been endlessly discussed since Descartes's own day, and is widely regarded as the inescapable flaw in dualism.[22]

---

21. Beloff, "The Mind-Brain Problem," 512.
22. Dennett, *Consciousness Explained*, 35.

Shortly after this he writes: "This fundamentally antiscientific stance of dualism is, to my mind, its most disqualifying feature, and is the reason why in this book I adopt the apparently dogmatic rule that dualism is to be avoided *at all costs*."[23]

Commenting on the argument Dennett presents, physicist Henry Stapp writes:

> The argument depends on identifying "standard physics" with classical physics. The argument collapses when one goes over to contemporary physics, in which trajectories of particles are replaced by cloud-like structures, and in which conscious choices can influence physically described activity without violating the conservation laws or any other laws of quantum mechanics. *Contemporary physical theory allows, and its orthodox von Neumann form entails, an interactive dualism that is fully in accord with all the laws of physics.*[24]

Physicists Rosenblum and Kuttner also reject Dennett's arguments:

> Some theorists deny the possibility of duality by arguing that a signal from a non-material mind could not carry energy and thus could not influence material brain cells. Because of this inability of a mind to supply energy to influence the neurons of the brain, it is claimed that physics demonstrates an inescapable flaw of dualism. However, no energy need be involved in determining to *which particular* situation a wavefunction collapses. Thus, the determination of which of the physically possible conscious experiences becomes the actual experience is a process that need not involve energy transfer. Quantum mechanics therefore allows an escape from the supposed fatal

---

23. Dennett, *Consciousness Explained*, 37.
24. Stapp, *Mindful Universe*, 81. Emphasis in original text.

flaw of dualism. It is a mistake to think that dualism can be ruled out on the basis of physics.[25]

Finally, although Dennett displays ignorance of modern physics, his objection does not even follow from anything in classical physics. For, as physicist-philosopher C. D. Broad pointed out decades ago, even if all physical-to-physical causation involves transfer of energy, we have no reason to think that such transfer would also be required in mental-to-physical or physical-to-mental causation.[26]

It was considerations such as these that led physicist-philosopher Nick Herbert to this shrewd dismissal of all the arguments against dualism:

> In this materialistic age, dualists are often accused of smuggling outmoded religious beliefs back into science, of introducing superfluous spiritual forces into biology, and of venerating an invisible "ghost in the machine." However, our utter ignorance concerning the real origins of human consciousness marks such criticism more a matter of taste than of logical thinking. At this stage of mind science, dualism is not irrational, merely somewhat unfashionable.[27]

In short, the transmission and production hypotheses are equally compatible with the facts that materialism tries to explain—such as the effects of senility, drugs, and brain damage on consciousness—but the transmission hypothesis has the clear advantage of being able to explain other phenomena that are utterly inexplicable by the hypothesis of production. These phenomena include, but are by no means restricted to, the evidence for survival that will be considered below.

---

25. Rosenblum and Kuttner, "Consciousness and Quantum Mechanics," 248.
26. Broad, *The Mind and Its Place in Nature*, 103.
27. Herbert, *Elemental Mind*, 23.

But before we consider the evidence for survival, let us first briefly consider some remarkable evidence from both biology and medicine that provide *prima facie* evidence indicating that the mind is not ultimately dependent on the brain.

Are Memories Stored in the Brain?

As mentioned above, some "skeptics" of survival insist that since memories are stored in the brain, memories cannot survive the destruction of the brain. But the idea that memories are stored in the brain is an assumption, not a fact, and there are some medical facts that call this assumption into serious question.

The idea that memories are somehow stored in the brain is an ancient idea; Aristotle, for instance, compared memories to impressions left in wax by seals. Over time, the analogies were updated to include tape recordings, and then more recently, to resemble computer memory storage.

However, modern attempts to locate memory traces in the brain have been spectacularly unsuccessful. For example, in one experiment, chicks were taught to perform a new task, and, using injections of radioactive material, resulting changes in the left hemisphere of their forebrains were noted, compared to chicks who did not undergo the training. However, when the new brain structures were removed, the chicks still remembered how to perform the task. The cells that had experienced greater growth as a result of the training were not necessary for memory retention. Similar experiments have been performed with rats, monkeys, chimpanzees, and octopuses, and yet even when up to 60 percent of the brains of the animals have been removed, the unfortunate animals could often still remember how to perform the recently learned task. Findings such as this have led at least one researcher to the untestable conclusion that "memory seems to be both everywhere and nowhere in particular."[28]

Maverick biologist Rupert Sheldrake has reviewed the extensive literature documenting the search for memory traces, and has concluded:

> There may be a ridiculously simple reason for these recurrent failures to find memory traces in brains: They may not exist. A search inside your TV set for traces of the programs you watched last week would be doomed to failure for the same reason: The set tunes in to TV transmissions but does not store them.
>
> But what about the fact that memories can be lost as a result of brain damage? Some types of damage in specific areas of the brain can result in specific kinds of impairment: for example, the loss of the ability to recognize faces after damage to the secondary visual cortex of the right hemisphere. A sufferer may fail to recognize the faces even of his wife and children, even though he can still recognize them by their voices and in other ways. Does this not prove that the relevant memories were stored inside the damaged tissues? By no means. Think again of the TV analogy. Damage to some parts of the circuitry can lead to loss or distortion of picture; damage to other parts can make the set lose the ability to produce sound; damage to the tuning circuit can lead to loss of the ability to receive one or more channels. But this does not prove that the pictures, sounds, and entire programs are stored inside the damaged components.[29]

---

28. Boycott, "Learning in the Octopus," 44.

29. Sheldrake, *The Rebirth of Nature*, 116–117.

Terminal Lucidity

For centuries medical practitioners have reported a strange phenomenon: in the days, hours, or minutes before death, patients suffering from profound mental impairment due to dementia or brain damage sometimes give every indication of recovering mental clarity and memories. In a recent paper on terminal lucidity Nahm and Greyson wrote: "In one study of end-of-life experiences, 70% of caregivers in a nursing home reported that during the past 5 years, they had observed patients with dementia becoming lucid a few days before death. Members of another palliative care team confirmed that such incidents happen regularly."[30]

Today, autopsies are usually only performed when foul play is suspected, or upon request from family members. However, decades ago autopsies were much more routinely performed. German biologist Michael Nahm extensively surveyed the European literature and found the following case first reported in 1921. G. W. Surya's friend's brother had been confined to an asylum for many years because of serious mental derangement.

> One day, Surya's friend received a telegram from the director of the asylum saying that his brother wanted to speak to him. He immediately visited his brother and was astonished to find him in a perfectly normal mental state. On leaving again, the director of the asylum decently informed the visitor that his brother's mental clarity is an almost certain sign of his approaching death. Indeed, the patient died within a short time. Subsequently, an autopsy of the brain was performed, to which Surya's friend was allowed to attend. It revealed that the brain was entirely suppurated and that this condition must have been present for a long time. Surya asks: "With what, then, did this

---

30. Nahm and Greyson, "Terminal Lucidity in Patients with Chronic Schizophrenia and Dementia," 943.

brainsick person think intelligibly again during the last days of his life?"[31]

A more recent case involves an elderly woman suffering from Alzheimer's disease, "largely caused by degeneration and irreversible degradation of the cerebral cortex and the hippocampus, resulting among other symptoms in confusion, disorientation, and memory loss."[32]

The woman had neither talked nor reacted to family members for years. And yet one week before she died, she suddenly started chatting with her granddaughter about various family members and giving her advice. Her granddaughter said that it was like talking to someone who had been asleep twenty years.[33]

Reports such as this suggest that the mind of the patient is disengaged, or disengaging, from the restrictions of a material brain. This conclusion is nothing new, as Nahm reminds us:

Hippocrates, Plutarch, Cicero, Galen, Avicenna, and other scholars of classical times noted that symptoms of mental disorders decrease as death approaches (du Prel, 1888/1971). All of them held the view that the soul remains basically intact when the brain is affected by physical malfunction and disturbance of the mind. Therefore, they believed that during and after death, the soul was freed from material constraints, regaining its full potential.[34]

---

31. Nahm, "Terminal Lucidity in People with Mental Illness and Other Mental Disability," 95.
32. Nahm and Greyson, "Terminal Lucidity in Patients with Chronic Schizophrenia and Dementia," 944.
33. Nahm et al., "Terminal Lucidity: A Review and a Case Collection," 140.
34. Nahm, "Terminal Lucidity in People with Mental Illness and Other Mental Disability," 90.

Conclusions

From the above it should be clear that the possibility of the survival of the mind following the death of the body cannot be dismissed on *a priori* grounds. The statement "the mind survives the death of the body" is not self-contradictory; nor is the idea in conflict with any of the facts or rules of nature as currently understood. Nor is it "simpler" to assume the brain produces the mind. There is neither any antecedent improbability of survival, nor is there any antecedent probability. This issue can only be settled by the testimony of the facts.

Chapter 2
The Nature of Evidence

What is evidence? In legal terms, it includes established facts and testimony from competent individuals that apparently have no motive to lie or embellish. Both types of evidence are considered reliable in court.

Reliability of Eyewitness Testimony

Some of the evidence that we will review, such as reports of apparitions, has been routinely dismissed on the grounds that they are based on eyewitness testimony, and that eyewitness testimony is notoriously unreliable. In support of this assertion, skeptics will often refer to experiments involving staged events in psychology classrooms. However, it is important to remember that although witnesses to an event, actual or staged, may disagree on incidental details, *they may all agree that such an event occurred*. That is, they may disagree on whether the assailant had red or brown hair, a green or blue shirt, fired two shots or three; and yet all may agree that a shooting occurred.

On this point, David Lorimer has written:

Recently the unreliability of human testimony has been the subject of psychological experiments in which a sequence of staged events suddenly takes place during a psychology lecture, and the students are asked to write a description. In many cases this proves to be inaccurate in its details, sometimes wildly so. The result of this is then used to justify a wholesale rejection of the validity of human testimony. But we do not take human testimony at its face value. The law has an elaborate procedure of cross-questioning of witnesses, whose accounts are expected to square with other facts pertinent to the case, including the alleged perpetrator's own description. If the testimony reveals a discrepancy, then this is followed up in turn, so that either a more comprehensive account is arrived at, or some part of the evidence or testimony is rejected. In the end there are generally a number of facts and testimonies which support a particular hypothesis as the most plausible account of the event, even if it is recognized that absolute certainty is ruled out.[35]

Yes, tragic errors have occurred in courtrooms because of mistaken eyewitness testimony. But this fact does not imply that *all* eyewitness testimony is seriously flawed, and that courts should therefore rule all such evidence inadmissible. Juries are only asked to decide based on guilt beyond *reasonable* doubt, not beyond all conceivable doubt. As mentioned above, the law has an elaborate system of verifying the accuracy of the core of eyewitness testimony; it is also important to remember that wrongful convictions are frequently overturned on appeal.

And just how reliable is eyewitness testimony *in real life*? Because of the unrealistic nature of staged events, the response of the judicial system to such studies has been lukewarm.[36] Staged

---

35. Lorimer, *Survival?*, 103.
36. Yuille and Cutshall, "A Case Study of Eyewitness Memory to a Crime," 291.

events cannot replicate the seriousness of actual events, and so psychologists Yuille and Cutshall examined an actual shooting. A gun store was robbed by an armed assailant, and the owner picked up a revolver and followed the robber into the street, where a shootout occurred in broad daylight, in full view of multiple bystanders.

Five months later, Yuille and Cutshall interviewed thirteen of the fifteen principal witnesses and compared their statements with the police reconstruction of the incident (this reconstruction was done by combining the eyewitness reports with photographs of the scene, location of bloodstains, reports from ambulance attendants, and forensic evidence) and with the statements the witnesses had given five months earlier. Yuille and Cutshall concluded:

> We take issue with the essentially negative view of the eyewitness that has been consistently presented by most eyewitness researchers ... In the present research ... a different picture emerges. Most of the witnesses in this case were highly accurate in their accounts, and this continued to be true 5 months after the event.[37]

Law professor Frederick Schauer agrees:

> It is true that neither memory nor first-person perception are as accurate as they have traditionally have been understood to be. And it is important that we know this, especially because of the consequences in the criminal justice system and occasionally elsewhere of the overvaluation of first-person or eyewitness accounts. Still, most—indeed, a lot more than most—eyewitness accounts are accurate. And most memories are accurate as well, providing evidence of what those describing what they have seen, heard, or experienced have in

---

37. Yuille and Cutshall, "A Case Study of Eyewitness Memory to a Crime," 299.

fact seen, heard, or experienced … That both perception and memory are often flawed is not inconsistent with perception and memory being even more often accurate and thus of evidentiary value.[38]

Anecdotal Evidence

Most of the evidence presented here could be considered as a collection of case studies, which some may consider a weakness. However, case studies are commonly published in medical journals, and are widely accepted as evidence by medical researchers. Yet, what about the criticism that case studies are only anecdotal, and therefore open to question?

A reviewer of one of my books on survival wrote:

> Unfortunately, case studies provide only anecdotal evidence—the weakest form of scientific support. Perhaps the greatest problem with anecdotal evidence is that it is based solely upon eyewitness testimony, and as extensive systematic research indicates, eyewitness testimony is highly prone to error. Carter provided a logical argument with anecdotal evidence, but such arguments and evidence have misled humanity in the past. For instance, before humans had circumnavigated the globe, there was a good solid argument, even supported by empirical data, that the earth was flat. Despite the quality of the argument and data, that hypothesis was wrong.[39]

With regard to the first point, we have seen that systematic research outside the narrow confines of the classroom indicates that eyewitness testimony in real-life situations can indeed be highly reliable. And with regard to the historical argument, long

---

38. Schauer, 2022, 131–2.
39. Hamrick, "Book Review: Science and the Afterlife Experience," 32.

before Magellan circumnavigated the globe, every educated person knew that the earth was round. Knowledge of the spherical shape of the earth was known at least as far back as Pythagoras; the ancients noted the shape of the earth's shadow upon the moon during an eclipse, and how the masts of approaching ships gradually appeared on the horizon. The best explanation for this data was that the earth was a sphere.

The word *anecdotal* comes from the Greek *anekdotos*, meaning "an unpublished story." So, when medical stories are published, they literally cease to be anecdotes, and are promoted to the status of case studies.

In medical research and other fields, anecdotal evidence may only be considered suggestive, not conclusive, *when we are trying to establish causal links between variables observed in repeatable events*. But when we are dealing with an unrepeatable event it is certainly possible to ask what is the best explanation for the event. Anecdotal evidence may thus be considered solid evidence *that* an event occurred, without by itself conclusively establishing the causal factors behind such an event.

It is sometimes said that anecdotal evidence is subjective—that is, peculiar to each individual. But, as mentioned above, the law has an elaborate system of cross-questioning witnesses, seeking a common core of testimony, and comparing this testimony with physical evidence, until an agreed-upon set of facts is reached as the most credible account. Those parts of testimony that are peculiar to individuals may thus be excluded.

As biologist Rupert Sheldrake writes,

> To brush aside what people have actually experienced is not to be scientific, but unscientific. Science is founded on the

empirical method, that is to say on experience and observation. Experiences and observations are the starting point for science, and it is unscientific to disregard or exclude them.[40]

And as we will see later, much of our evidence for survival does *not* rely on eyewitness testimony, and is in fact *permanent and objective*.

Inference to the Best Explanation

An inference is, of course, a conclusion that is formed because of known facts or evidence; the term also refers to the *process* of inferring, that is, of examining evidence to draw a conclusion. When, in medical or scientific research, we are trying to establish causal links between variables that can be observed in repeatable events—such as between cancer survival rates and a certain medication—then experiments are ideally performed. In medical research, the gold standard is the double-blind experiment, in which as many causal variables as possible are controlled in order to determine if there really is an effect, and if so, of what magnitude.

However, as Oxford professor of mathematics and philosophy of science John Lennox writes:

> We do not always have the luxury of repeated observation or experimentation. We cannot repeat the Big Bang, or the origin of life, or the history of life, or the history of the universe. Indeed, what about any historical event? It is not repeatable. Does that mean we can say nothing about such things? There is, however, another methodology that can be applied to such situations, well known to historians. It is the method of inference to the best explanation.[41]

---

40. Sheldrake, *The Sense of Being Stared At*, 5.
41. Lennox, *God's Undertaker?*, 85.

This is a method of practical reasoning commonly used in daily life, and by historians, police detectives, lawyers in courtrooms, and research scientists. When there are several logically possible explanations, more evidence is gathered until only one explanation remains that is consistent with *all* the known facts. An explanation that is proven false by one or more known facts cannot be the best explanation, and as Lennox adds, "an argument that does explain a given effect is always better than one that does not."[42]

42. Lennox, *God's Undertaker?*, 85.

Chapter 3
Standards of Proof

In legal matters there are two main standards of proof. In the majority of civil cases, the plaintiff must prove only that the *preponderance of evidence* is on their side; that is, that all the evidence, considered as a whole, indicates that their claim is more likely true than not. Criminal cases are held to a more demanding standard: the prosecution must prove *beyond all reasonable doubt* that the defendant is guilty as charged.

In all empirical matters, the strongest case we can make is proof beyond all reasonable doubt; only in pure logic and mathematics can we prove statements *beyond all conceivable doubt*. Consider the purely abstract argument: If A > B, and B > C, then A *must be* > C. It is simply inconceivable that C > A. Only in matters of abstract logic can we attain certainty beyond all conceivable doubt; but this comes at the expense of saying nothing about the world.[43] When dealing with factual matters, we can never reach conclusions with mathematical certainty.

---

43. With one sole exception: Descartes's *I think, therefore I exist*.

But what exactly do we mean by the standard of proof beyond all reasonable doubt? Ultimately, it must mean this: an assertion is proven beyond all reasonable doubt when we have good reason to believe it is true, *and* we have no good reason to believe it may *not* be true. And in all empirical matters, "good reasons" are those based upon reliable evidence.

Let us examine this further.

In criminal trials, the rules of evidence prohibit both prosecution and defense from arguing on the basis of speculation, on the grounds that no one should be convicted or acquitted on the basis of speculation. Only arguments based upon evidence are allowed.

In legal terms *prima facie* (Latin for "first look") evidence refers to evidence that is sufficient to prove the case, unless convincing evidence to the contrary can be shown. Before a criminal case can be brought to trial, the burden of proof lies with the prosecution to present evidence to a grand jury that makes a strong *prima facie* case for guilt. The reason for this burden is the principle that suspects are presumed innocent until proven guilty, and the prosecution's job is to convince a grand jury that, in this case, the presumption of innocence is not justified, and a trial is therefore warranted. Of course, once trial begins, the prosecution must prove that the accused is guilty beyond any reasonable doubt.

A defense lawyer's job during trial is to raise reasonable doubt in the minds of the jury. If during trial it becomes apparent that the strategy of the defense is to offer an alternate theory of the crime that has no evidential basis, then the prosecutor will object on the grounds that the alternate theory is pure speculation, unsupported by evidence. And according to the rules of evidence, any judge doing their duty will sustain the objection, because a mere logical possibility without supporting evidence is not considered a basis for reasonable doubt.

Of course, in practice defense lawyers will sometimes try any form of sophistry in an attempt to raise the illusion of reasonable doubt in the minds of a jury. Jurors are human, and as such, are often influenced by appeals to emotions such as sympathy, anger, fear of the police, and so on. When strong emotions are aroused, clear thinking is difficult, and so a clever defense lawyer can use this technique to convince a jury that a mere logical possibility— such as police corruption—is in fact a real possibility, even in the absence of any positive evidence in support.

We may on occasion expect such sophistry from defense lawyers, as their earnings depend upon their success in winning cases. Even so, mere speculation unsupported by evidence is not admissible in a court of law, and an effective prosecutor will raise an objection every time such sophistry is attempted.

The most demanding concept of proof in legal matters—as in all empirical matters—is that of proof beyond all *reasonable* doubt, not proof beyond all *conceivable* doubt. Only in mathematics and pure logic can we prove anything beyond all conceivable doubt. This is the reason speculative arguments from the defense are forbidden in courtrooms by the rules of evidence: speculative arguments with no evidential basis raise the burden of proof on the prosecution from beyond all reasonable doubt to beyond all conceivable doubt, an impossible standard to meet in factual matters.

Placing the burden of proof upon those making a claim is one means by which speculation is, ideally, kept out of any dispute over factual matters, whether inside or outside of court. The obligation of both parties to provide solid evidence in support of their claims is essential in any attempt to resolve matters of fact beyond reasonable, as opposed to conceivable, doubt.

In our discussion of the evidence, I will present a strong *prima facie* case that survival of consciousness past the point of bodily death has been proven beyond all reasonable doubt. Various skeptical attempts to raise reasonable doubt are then critically examined.

Real versus Imaginary Possibilities

The distinction between evidence and speculation can be better understood by distinguishing between real and imaginary possibilities. Let us elaborate on this distinction, because—as we will see later in our discussion of the skeptical objections—this distinction is crucial.

A purely logical possibility is any that can be stated without self-contradiction: for instance, the possibility raised by the philosopher René Descartes that we and the world were created by an evil demon only minutes ago, complete with memories of the past. A modern update on this idea was presented in the science fiction film *The Matrix*. But a logical possibility is not a real possibility unless there is some reason to believe it may actually be true.

Note that there are two different types of imaginary or purely logical possibilities: (1) those of which we have examples of them having occurred in the past, but no evidence that they occurred in this case (for instance, we may agree that historically, corrupt police have in fact planted evidence), and (2) those for which there is no reason to *ever* seriously entertain as real possibilities (such as police planting false memories in the minds of witnesses: there is simply no reason to believe that corrupt police officers are even *capable* of employing such vast powers).

Real possibilities are supported by evidence; imaginary possibilities are simply pure speculation. Only real possibilities can provide rational reasons to believe that a factual claim is or is not true.

The Extraordinary Claims Objection

This objection, usually attributed to astronomer Carl Sagan, simply states that extraordinary claims require extraordinary evidence. But we need to remember that we have no objective guidelines as to what counts as an "extraordinary" claim, and no objective criteria for what counts as "extraordinary evidence." And several claims that were once considered truly extraordinary are now commonly accepted by elementary school children around the world. These would include the claim that rocks sometimes fall from the sky (what we today call meteorites), the claim that the continents drift (ridiculed by many geologists for decades), and the claim that washing hands before assisting in childbirth or practicing surgery greatly reduces the risk of subsequent death by infection. Evidence *that* these phenomena occurred was routinely mocked and ridiculed, because the experts of the day could not explain *how* these phenomena could occur.

Chapter 4
The Nature of Science

Science is concerned with theories, but in science the term "theory" means something different that it does in ordinary conversation. In police work, for instance, "theory" may only mean a provisional explanation for a crime. In science it refers to an explanation in terms of variables, and describes how two or more variables relate to each other. An example is Newton's theory of universal gravitation, which relates the force of gravity between a planet and the sun to the product of their masses and the square of the distance between them.

Note that the modern term is theory, not *law*. The term "law of nature" is an anachronism, dating back to the time when scientists and philosophers believed that Newton's theories were facts of nature, not merely provisional approximations to the truth. Today, we speak of Newton's laws and Einstein's theories, even though Einstein's theories are more accurate approximations to reality than Newton's so-called laws (Einstein quickly became a world-famous celebrity among the general public in 1919 after the demonstration during an eclipse that his theory of gravity more accurately than Newton's predicted the bending of starlight by a massive body).

As a student, the philosopher Karl Popper attended an early lecture by Einstein and was greatly impressed by Einstein's admission that although his theory of gravity made more accurate predictions than Newton's, *it was not actually true*, but merely a better approximation. This led Popper to devote much of his career developing his philosophy of science, which in turn was admired and endorsed by Einstein.

Popper's work is a refutation of Hume's conclusion that our "laws of nature" are general conclusions based upon repeated observation of specific instances (that is, inductions) and are therefore not rational. Suppose, for instance, that every swan we have ever seen has been white, and we then conclude that "all swans are white." This is a (simple) scientific theory that relates two variables to each other. But is it valid reasoning to treat this statement as a law of nature? No, said Hume, because induction is not a valid method of reasoning: after all, the very next swan we see may be black.

This conclusion greatly troubled the philosopher Bertrand Russell, as he was unable to solve the problem. Russell was forced to conclude that if we are to practice science then we have no choice but to accept "induction is an independent logical principle, incapable of being inferred either from experience or from other logical principles, and that without this principle science is impossible."[44] Russell's desperate solution is essentially to accept Hume's logical refutation of induction, but then to argue that we must accept it as a principle incapable of being justified by logic or experience, or in other words, simply on faith. Otherwise, "science is impossible."

---

44. Russell, *A History of Western Philosophy*, 647.

Popper's solution was radically different: he denied that induction is needed in science if we treat our ideas not as "laws" but merely as theories, hypotheses, approximations to the truth. Although we can never prove our scientific theories true—no matter how many white swans we see, the next one may well be black—one black swan disproves the theory that all swans are white.

Thus, Popper was led to his criterion of testability; according to Popper, "a theory is scientific to the *degree* it is testable."[45] And because induction has no validity, testing of a scientific theory can only mean attempts to prove false, not correct.[46] Popper's method provides science with a means for learning from its mistakes, and thus provides science with a self-corrective mechanism at its core.

Our analysis of the data for survival is similar to that of a prosecuting attorney in a criminal case: we critically examine all the evidence in order to infer the best explanation for the facts. Unlike scientific theories, statements regarding *specific factual matters* are often capable of being proven false *or correct* beyond all reasonable doubt (such as the statement "this bird is a black swan"). The main relevance here for Popper's criterion is its delineation of scientific theories as distinct from metaphysical or ideological theories. Scientific theories are capable of being tested—that is, falsified; metaphysical theories are not, because of the absence or scarcity of available evidence. If they eventually become capable of being tested, then they are "kicked upstairs" and become part of science. (Some critics complain that Popper's theory is not itself testable, missing the point that it is not meant to be a scientific theory. It is a *methodology* that describes how science may advance by learning from its mistakes.)

---

45. Popper, "Replies to my Critics," 981.
46. This discussion is very brief; a much more detailed discussion can be found in chapter 15 of *Science and Psychic Phenomena* (formerly titled *Parapsychology and the Skeptics*).

But the reverse may happen: a scientific theory may be refuted by the data, and its supporters may then try to salvage it with the addition of auxiliary assumptions; if these render the theory untestable, it ceases to be science and becomes ideology. Popper argued forcefully that this happened with Marxist theory, which made certain key testable predictions—it predicted that capitalism would lead to increasing poverty and misery for the majority, leading to a communist revolution in the more developed capitalist societies. When the revolution first occurred in then-backward and agrarian Russia, its supporters did not take this fact as a refutation; instead, they modified the theory so that it became immune from falsification. A scientific theory with testable predictions thus became an ideology, maintained simply because of social and political agendas.

Given the horrors that were unleashed upon the world during the twentieth century as direct results of the ideologies of communism and fascism, it should be evident that any testable theory that has been rendered unfalsifiable in order to be sustained is unworthy of serious consideration.

The hypothesis of living-agent ESP claims that extrasensory perception can explain certain things. In its testable form, it may be considered a scientific theory, capable of being refuted by the data.

If after falsification in its testable form its supporters then defend it with the addition of various untestable *ad hoc* assumptions, then the theory has been immunized from falsification, and has been transformed into the unfalsifiable ideology of *Super*-ESP.

Part II
The Evidence

If you have finished Part I, then you now have all the tools necessary to deal with the most common skeptical objections to the evidence. In Part II, we consider that evidence, focusing on several of the most compelling cases from five independent lines of evidence. The emphasis here will be on *why* these cases are so compelling. Ultimately, the reason is because they cannot be explained by fraud, human error, or by any form of perception, *normal or extrasensory (super or otherwise)*.

We will see that only the theory of Super-ESP remains in the field to challenge the inference of survival.

Chapter 5

The Near-Death Experience

One phenomenon that would appear to be able to shed light on the relationship between mind and body would be the near-death experience (NDE), in which people revived after experiencing clinical death often report unusual, lucid experiences. It is estimated that now over 300 million worldwide have reported such experiences.[47] Published studies by cardiologists have reported that, when asked, between 10 percent and 18 percent of patients recovering from cardiac arrest will report an NDE.[48]

Although scattered reports of NDEs appear throughout history, systematic study of the NDE only began in the 1970s, with the publication of the book *Life After Life* by physician Raymond Moody. Here is Moody's composite description:

> A man is dying and, as he reaches the point of greatest physical distress, he hears himself pronounced dead by his doctor. He begins to feel himself moving very rapidly through a long dark tunnel. After this, he suddenly finds himself outside of his own physical body, but still in the

---

47. Personal communication, NDE researcher Bruce Greyson, MD, June 1, 2021.
48. Carter, *Science and the Near-Death Experience*, 104.

immediate physical environment, and he sees his own body from a distance, as though he is a spectator. He watches the resuscitation attempt from this unusual vantage point.

After a while, he collects himself. He notices that he still has a "body", but one of a very different nature and with very different powers from the physical body he has left behind. Soon other things begin to happen. Others come to meet and help him. He glimpses the spirits of relatives and friends who have already died, and a loving, warm spirit of a kind he never encountered before—a being of light—appears before him. This being asks him a question, nonverbally, to make him evaluate his life and helps him by showing him a panoramic, instantaneous playback of the major events of his life. At some point he finds himself approaching some sort of barrier or border, apparently representing the limit between earthly life and the next life. Yet, he finds that he must go back to earth, that the time for his death has not yet come. At this point, he resists, for by now he is taken up with his experiences in the afterlife and does not want to return. He is overwhelmed by intense feelings of joy, love, and peace. Despite his attitude, though, he somehow reunites with his physical body and lives.

The experience affects his life profoundly, especially his views about death and its relationship to life.[49]

The table below shows the frequency with which the various stages have been reported, in five independent medical studies of roughly the same size.[50]

---

49. Moody, *Life After Life*, 21.
50. Carter, *Science and the Near-Death Experience*, 109.

Stages of the Western NDE
(Weighted Averages)

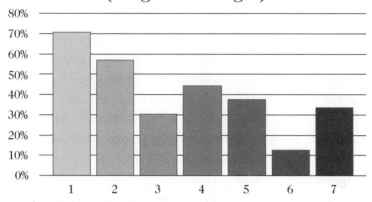

1. Peace or joy
2. Out-of-body experience (OBE)
3. Entering a tunnel or darkness
4. Encountering a light
5. Meeting the deceased or a being
6. Life review
7. Unearthly realm

Of the various stages, the OBE arguably provides the most important evidence that the mind can function apart from the physical brain. Some of those who recall leaving their physical body perceive themselves existing as disembodied consciousness, while others report that while they were "outside," they had a new, bodylike form.

The unusual properties of this body are illustrated in this account:

People were walking up from all directions to get to the wreck. I could see them, and I was in the middle of a very narrow walkway. Anyway, as they came by they wouldn't seem to notice me.

They would just keep walking with their eyes straight ahead. As they came real close, I would try to turn around, to get out of their way, but they would just walk *through* me.[51]

Those who experience the separation report that their mental processes are clear, sharp, and rational—if anything, they report being able to think faster and more clearly than ever. Vision and hearing are usually the only two senses reported, and these are often described as enhanced to an incredible degree.[52] Panoramic, 360-degree vision is sometimes reported, and some individuals claim they could see through walls and other objects. The ability to read people's thoughts telepathically is sometimes mentioned. In movement there seems to be weightlessness, and an ability to project themselves wherever they want.

Here is an example:

In 1986 I was rushed into Bradford Royal Infirmary and underwent emergency surgery. I spent five weeks in intensive care, then a further four months in a ward. My experience of death was wonderful. I was floating high up, no pain, great joy, and no fear. Down a tunnel with a very bright light at the end. Animals, pictures, everything was so beautiful and all the colours were shades of delicate pink, yellow, blue, etc. I was overwhelmed with joy. I truly believe I as on the brink of death. I cannot have made up a story like this. I was told a long time afterwards by my relatives that I *did* die and the moment of entering the intensive care unit, but it was not to be. I heard my dad's voice calling me back. I was on the critical list. No hope was given to my family and now here I am with my life. My experience has had a profound effect on my life. I thank the

---

51. Valarino, 45, from Raymond Moody's *Life After Life*.
52. NDEs involving vision have also been reported by the blind, and Appendix II contains one such firsthand account.

Lord for every new day, but if death is the wonderful experience I had, I'm not afraid of death.[53]

Commenting on this and similar cases, cardiologist Peter Fenwick writes, "Not only do people see, hear, and smell in the NDE, but their perceptions seem to be heightened. When music is heard it is 'heavenly,' colours are 'beautiful,' 'vivid,' 'unearthly': smells are usually described as 'beautiful,' 'summery,' 'flowery.'"[54]

Most of the individuals who have reported an NDE consider it to have been the single most pivotal event of their lives. The nature of the NDE may be controversial, but there is no doubt of the aftereffects, which typically include increased compassion for others, reduced interest in material possessions, and an increased appreciation for life, coupled with a greatly reduced fear of death.

Alternative Explanations

Several alternative explanations have been proposed, and next we will carefully examine the two top contenders.

Oxygen Deprivation

Perhaps the most common materialist explanations for the NDE is either a complete lack of oxygen (anoxia) or a reduced supply (hypoxia). The effects of both are well-known: anoxia—as experienced during cardiac arrest—causes unconsciousness in seconds; hypoxia—as sometimes experienced during a heart attack—causes a series of subjective phenomena as the subject's brain becomes increasingly hypoxic.

Mountain climbers have frequently experienced hypoxia, as have pilots flying at high altitude. Symptoms typically include mental laziness, slowness in reasoning, and difficulty in remembering.

---

53. Fenwick and Fenwick, *The Truth in the Light*, 84.
54. Fenwick and Fenwick, *The Truth in the Light*, 84.

When the brain is starved for oxygen—as for instance, when air pressure is suddenly lost inside a flight cabin—a person has only a very short time before consciousness is lost. This is why the pre-flight instructions on an aircraft ask you to don your own oxygen mask before attending to the dependent child beside you. Pilots in training regularly undergo acute anoxia in flight simulators to make sure they can get their masks on in time. Those who fail do not have NDEs: they experience confusion and disorientation, sometimes trying to land their simulated planes on top of clouds before losing consciousness.

We have the report of a man who has experienced both anoxia and the tunnel while near death. While he was an RAF pilot, Allan Pring experienced anoxia at high altitude, and years later he had an NDE:

> I found myself "floating" along in a dark tunnel, peacefully and calmly but wide awake and aware. I know that the tunnel experience has been attributed to the brain being deprived of oxygen, but as an ex-pilot who has experienced lack of oxygen at altitude I can state that for me there was no similarity. On the contrary, the whole [NDE] experience from beginning to end was crystal clear and it has remained so for the past fifteen years.[55]

Hypoxia has also been induced in laboratory experiments. Years ago, it was common practice for medical students to be shown the effects of depriving their brains of oxygen. Students were told to breathe through a carbon dioxide absorber into and out of a spirometer filled with air. While doing this they were given some simple task to perform. Breathing through this apparatus ensured that carbon dioxide was absorbed and was not allowed

---

to build up in the students' blood, and so the students would not realize that they were slowly suffocating. They would continue to breathe normally, unaware that the air they were breathing contained less and less oxygen. Their performance at the task would become increasingly inept, until eventually they lost consciousness. In thousands of such experiments on thousands of people, no one ever reported a near-death experience.

This disorientation and confusion contrasts sharply with the clarity of thought and perception reported again and again in accounts of the NDE.

In my second book, *Science and the Near-Death Experience*, I considered every proposed physiological and psychological counter-explanation for the NDE that I could find, and *not one* stood up to critical scrutiny. All that is left to consider is the possibility of an explanation due to extrasensory perception.

Clairvoyance (ESP)

Some have proposed that any OBE during an NDE that includes accurate perception of the surroundings is due to clairvoyant perception, occurring either before the patient loses or after the patient regains consciousness. However, there are several problems with this idea.

First of all, simple clairvoyance is not enough: since patients report events that occurred during the moments they were unconscious, the clairvoyance must either be of the near future or the recent past. In other words, the explanation also requires the addition of at least one other form of ESP: either precognition or retrocognition. The problem with this is that any sort of insult to the brain results in a period of amnesia preceding *and* following the insult. This is also typically true in cases of NDE; and yet in the middle of the patients' amnesia is a crystal clear memory of an NDE with an OBE.

Secondly, clairvoyant descriptions are not typically from an elevated perspective, and certainly not from an elevated position directly above the viewer's own body. An even stronger objection is that these perceptions occurred when we have every reason to believe that the subjects' cerebral processes were either severely impaired or entirely absent.

Finally, clairvoyant perceptions are certainly not accompanied by the thought that one has died, feelings of peace and joy, lasting changes in values, and a greatly reduced fear of death.

Next, we consider two remarkable cases, and the "skeptical" attempts to explain them.

Lloyd Rudy's Patient

The following remarkable case was described in an interview with the famous American heart surgeon Lloyd Rudy.[56] Rudy described a patient who, on Christmas Day, needed emergency heart surgery to treat a severe infection of his heart valve. This exceptionally significant case was described and analyzed in great detail by Rivas, Dirven, and Smit in their comprehensive book *The Self Does Not Die*.

The following is mostly taken directly from this book. The first part is a transcript of the interview, and the remainder is the extremely thorough analysis of the case provided by Rivas, Dirven, and Smit.

> RUDY: We had a very unfortunate individual who on Christmas Day had, from an oral infection, infected his native

---

56. Retrieved from http://oralsystemiclink.pro/heart-attack-stroke/1st-scientific-session-of-the-academy-for-oral-systemichealth/.

valve ["native" referring to the patient's biological valve rather than an artificial, prosthetic valve]. If your native valve has the slightest defect, whether you were born with it or you developed it later—it calcified a little and the valve leaflets don't move or whatever—the body recognizes that as something abnormal. So that's what happened to this man, and one of my junior partners was on call, and he had to do an emergency valve resection. Once we were able to accomplish the repair of the aneurysm and the replacement of the valve, we could not get this person off of the bypass. Every time the four or five liters of blood that we were pumping around his body we would reduce down to two or three, he'd begin to weaken and his blood pressure would go down, and so on. To make a long story short: We simply couldn't get him off the heart-lung machine. Finally, we just had to give up. I mean, we just said: We cannot get him off of the heart-lung machine, so we're going to have to pronounce him dead. So, we did that.

And so, the anesthesiologist turned his machine off and the bellows that were breathing for the patient stopped. That machine was quiet. The anesthesiologist went into the surgeon's lounge. He hadn't eaten anything all day so he went in to have a sandwich. Then the people who usually clean up the instruments were coming in and taking away all these tools. And my surgical assistant closed the patient in a way that a postmortem exam could be done, because anyone who succumbs on the table, by law, has to have an autopsy. So, he closed him up briefly, with a couple or three wires here and a big stitch to close his soft tissue.

Well, that machine that records the blood pressure and the pulse and the left atrial pressure and all the monitoring lines and things continued to run the paper out onto the floor in a big heap. Nobody bothered to turn it off. And then we put down a trans-esophageal echo-probe, which is just a long tube that has a microphone on the end of it, and we can get a beautiful picture on a monitor of the heart beating. Well, that machine was left on, and the VCR-tape continued to run.

The assistant surgeon and I went in and took our gowns off, and gloves and masks, and came back, and we were in our short-sleeve shirts, and we were standing at the door, kind of discussing if there was anything else we could have done, any other medicines we could have given, to have made this a success. And as we were standing there—it had been at least 20 minutes. You know, I don't know this exact time sequence, but it was close to 20, 25 minutes, that this man recorded no heartbeat, no blood pressure [gestures to indicate the monitoring machine's continuous paper read-out], and the echo showing no movement of the heart, just sitting there.

And all of a sudden, we looked up—and this surgical assistant had just finished closing him—and we saw some electrical activity. And pretty soon, the electrical activity turned into a heartbeat. Very slow, 30, 40 [beats] a minute. And we thought, "Well, that's kind of an agonal thing"— and we see that, occasionally, that the heart will continue to beat even though the patient can't generate a blood pressure or pump any blood. Well, pretty soon we look, and he's actually generating a pressure. Now, we're not doing anything; I mean, the machines are all shut off. And we'd stopped all the medicines, and all that. And so I start yelling, "Get anesthesia back in here!" and, "Get the nurses!" And to make a very long story short, without putting him back on cardiopulmonary bypass—a heart-lung machine—we started giving him some medicines, and anesthesia started giving him oxygen. And pretty soon he had a blood pressure of 80, and pretty soon a blood pressure of 100, and his heart rate was now up to 100 a minute.

He recovered and had no neurologic deficit. And for the next 10 days, two weeks, all of us went in and were talking to him about what he experienced, if anything. And he talked about the bright light at the end of the tunnel, as I recall, and so on. But the thing that astounded me was that he described that operating room, floating around, and saying, "I saw you and Dr. Cattaneo standing in the doorway with your arms folded, talking. I didn't know where the anesthesiologist was, but he came running back in. And I saw all of these Post-its sitting on this TV screen."

And what those were, were any call I got, the nurse would write down who called and the phone number and stick it on the monitor, and then the next Post-it would stick to that Post-it, and then I'd have a string of Post-its of phone calls I had to make. He described that. I mean, there is no way he could have described that before the operation, because I didn't have any calls, right?

MILLIGAN: No, and he's sitting, he's lying on the [gestures to indicate surgical table]—so he must have been floating?

RUDY: He was up there. He described the scene, things that there is no way he knew. I mean, he didn't wake up in the operating room and see all this stuff.

MILLIGAN: No.

RUDY: I mean he was out. And was out for, I don't know, even a day or two while we recovered him in the intensive care unit. So, what does that tell you? Was that his soul up there?

MILLIGAN: It's hard to know, but it certainly brings that possibility into play.

RUDY: It always makes me very emotional.

On January 23, 2013, British correspondent Stephen Woodhead pointed out to Rudolf Smit an online comment by the cardiac surgeon Roberto Amado-Cattaneo of Great Falls, known as Dr. Cattaneo to his U.S. colleagues. In response to the video in which Rudy talked about the case, Dr. Amado-Cattaneo wrote:

> Dr. Rudy's description of this event at the time of this patient's surgery is absolutely correct. I was the other cardiac surgeon that he refers to in the video. The patient's description of his experience is as Dr. Rudy described it word by word. People should interpret this according to their own beliefs, these are the facts.

On January 28, 2013, Titus Rivas contacted Amado-Cattaneo by email and, in consultation with two NDE researchers, former International Association for Near-Death Studies (IANDS) president Jan Holden and psychiatrist Bruce Greyson, asked him a number of questions between the end of January and mid-February. Amado-Cattaneo wrote Rivas back the following:

> This case happened sometime late 1990's early 2000's. I do not know the patient's identity anymore. Neither do I think we can find out, unfortunately. It has been too long and I do not have any records of that case anymore. My role was that of assistant surgeon. I was in the case from beginning to end. I did witness the entire case and everything that my partner Dr. Rudy explained in the video. I do not have a rational scientific explanation to explain this phenomenon. I do know that this happened.
>
> This patient had close to 20 minutes or more of no life, no physiologic life, no heartbeat, no blood pressure, no respiratory function whatsoever and then he came back to life and told us what you heard on the video. He recovered fully. I do not think there was something wrong with the monitoring devices. The reason is that there are different types of monitors and they were left on. We could see a flatline, the monitor was on but

not recording electrical activity in the heart. When he started coming back, we could see at first a slow beat that eventually evolved into something really closer to normal. The same with the ultrasound scan placed inside the esophagus, we saw no heart activity for the 20 minutes or so, machine still on, and then it started showing muscle movement, that is, contractility of the heart muscle that eventually turned into close to normal function, able to generate a blood pressure and life. The reason we saw him coming back is that fact, that the monitors were on and so we saw him regaining life, when this happened we restarted full support with drugs, oxygen etc.

This was not a hoax, no way, this was as real as it gets. We were absolutely shocked that he would come back after 20 or more minutes, we had pronounced him dead on the operating room table and told the wife that he had died. I have seen people recover from profound and prolonged shock, but still having life, in this case there was no life. (R. Amado-Cattaneo, personal communication, January 28 and 30, 2013)

Subsequently, Rivas sent Amado-Cattaneo several additional questions suggested to him by Holden and Greyson about the veracity and normal explicability of the patient's statements and about the location of the monitor with the Post-it messages, respectively. Amado-Cattaneo replied:

I do not believe he said anything that we questioned as being real, we thought all along his description was quite accurate regarding things he said he saw or heard. Patients' eyes are always shut during surgery, most of the time they are taped so they do not open since this can cause injury to the corneas. (R. Amado-Cattaneo, personal communication, February 13, 2013)

>There are many [pieces of] non-sterile equipment in an operating room including monitors. Monitors are close range so surgeons can "monitor different parameters through the case." The messages to Dr. Rudy I believe were taped to a monitor that sits close to the end of the operating table, up in the air, close enough for anybody to see what is there, like the patient, for example, if he was looking at it. (Dr. R. Amado-Cattaneo, personal communication, February 15, 2013)

At the end of January 2013, Amado-Cattaneo told Smit's correspondent, Woodhead, that the case had occurred in the period that he and Lloyd Rudy had worked at the Deaconess Hospital in Spokane, Washington.[57]

Anesthesiologist Gerald Woerlee attempted to dismiss this case in an online article, as one that could be fit perfectly into his materialistic worldview. He invoked what he called "an unusual medical event called the [sic] 'The Lazarus Phenomenon,'" which he described as "a situation where a person spontaneously recovers heartbeat, blood pressure, breathing, and consciousness after periods of absent heartbeat … So this fascinating report by Lloyd Rudy is one of the rare, but known cases of the [sic] 'The Lazarus Phenomenon.'"[58]

I wrote to psychiatry professor Bruce Greyson, who has spent decades studying the NDE. He replied:

>To my knowledge, the Lazarus syndrome is not a proper diagnosis. The term is used to describe people who suffer a cardiac arrest but then recover spontaneously without resuscitation efforts and with no known cause. Calling something an exam-

---

57. Rivas, Dirven, and Smit, *The Self Does Not Die*, Case 3.11, 90–94.
58. Learn more at https://web.archive.org/web/20230405175406/http://www.neardth.com/lazarus.php.

ple of the Lazarus phenomenon does not explain it, but in fact states that we can't explain it.[59]

I also wrote to cardiologist Pim van Lommel, who has also conducted extensive medical research on the NDE.

As far as I know the "Lazarus phenomenon" is not an accepted medical terminology. It is a description of what has happened when someone is declared dead, or is believed to be dead, and then regains consciousness without any obvious medical explanation, and without any medical intervention.

The fact that this patient did not have problems with his short-term memory afterwards, and that he recovered so quickly despite not having had a heartbeat for about 20 minutes, must be explained by the fact that he had an NDE.[60]

Amado-Cattaneo agreed:

Dr. Woerlee's explanation does not apply to this case. This was not the Lazarus phenomenon, this patient was dead for 25 minutes or more with no cardiac pulmonary movement or brain function. The brain dies after a few minutes of lack of oxygen, period! This case was 25 minutes at least if not more. I cannot explain it, but it happened and I am a living witness of this case, I was there. Many times in medicine we just do not have the right answers or any answers. One can believe what one wants to believe but this in my mind is a miracle unexplainable by current scientific knowledge.

Regards,

Dr. Roberto Amado-Cattaneo

---

59. Personal communication, April 11, 2024.
60. Personal communication, April 12, 2024.

On September 16, 2015, Amado-Cattaneo sent Woodhead another email in response to the question of whether the patient might have been able to perceive something with his physical eyes without anyone noticing. Had they, perhaps, already removed the tape from his eyes? If so, what were the implications, then, regarding the question of whether or not his veridical observations could be determined to be normal?

Amado-Cattaneo wrote:

> We always remove the tapes at the end of the surgery before the patient is transferred to ICU. I am sure this was the case and if so he was so out loaded with anesthetics and other sedatives, that there is no way in the world that he could have seen or be aware of anything.[61]

Next, we consider one of the deepest NDEs ever reported.

Operation Standstill

This case occurred during neurosurgery at the Barrow Neurological Institute in Phoenix Arizona on an August morning in 1991. Thirty-five-year-old Pam Reynolds was being operated on for a giant aneurysm in the wall of an artery located at the base of her brain, which had ballooned out and threatened to rupture. Dr. Robert Spetzler of the Barrow Institute had pioneered a daring surgical procedure known as hypothermic cardiac arrest that would allow Pam's aneurysm to be removed. This operation, nicknamed "standstill," would require her body temperature to be lowered to 60 degrees Fahrenheit, her heartbeat and breathing stopped, the electrical activity in her brain extinguished, and the blood drained from her body. In ordinary clinical terms, Pam would be dead.

---

61. Rivas, Dirven, and Smit, *The Self Does Not Die*, 95.

This extraordinary episode in the history of NDE research is described in great detail by Michael Sabom in his book *Light and Death*. As Dr. Sabom notes, the medical documentation of the events surrounding this case *"far exceeds* any recorded before and provides us with our most complete scientific glimpse yet into the near-death experience."[62]

Pam was given general anesthesia, and instruments were set up to monitor heartbeat, brain activity in the cerebral cortex, and activity in the brain stem, the most primitive part of the brain, which controls involuntary functions such as breathing and reflexes such as pupil dilation. Brain stem activity was monitored by speakers inserted into her ears, which emitted 11 clicks per second at 95 to 100 decibels, considered at the threshold of causing hearing damage. Furthermore, earbuds were molded to fill her ear canals and covered with gauze to keep them in place, completely blocking out all other sound. Her eyes were taped shut, and Operation Standstill began.

By three clinical tests—flat EEG, no brainstem activity, no blood flowing through the brain—Pam's brain was dead, with almost certainly no activity whatsoever. Yet Pam reported the *deepest* near-death experience ever reported, including accurate, detailed perception of the operating room and an encounter with several deceased relatives.

According to Pam, her experience began as Spetzler started opening her skull with a pneumatically powered bone saw. She recalls leaving her body:

> I remember seeing several things in the operating room when I was looking down. It was the most aware that I think I have ever been in my entire life...It was not like normal vision.

---

62. Sabom, *Light and Death*, 38.

It was brighter and more focused and clearer than normal vision…There was so much in the operating room that I didn't recognize, and so many people.[63]

Pam correctly described the appearance of the bone saw ("like an electric toothbrush"), and correctly overheard spoken remarks made during the operation. Speaking on camera during the BBC documentary *The Day I Died*, lead surgeon Robert Spetzler described how:

At that stage of the operation nobody can observe or hear in that state. And I find it inconceivable that your normal senses, such as hearing—let alone the fact that she had clicking modules in each ear—that there was any way for her to hear through normal auditory pathways.

After cutting through the outermost membrane of her brain, Spetzler located the aneurysm, and as feared, it turned out to be large and extended into Pam's brain. Unfortunately, the risky procedure of hypothermic cardiac arrest (Operation Standstill) would be needed.

Pam's body temperature was cooled to 10 degrees Celsius (50 degrees Fahrenheit), severe hypothermia, which always induces cardiac arrest. As Pam's heart stopped, brain waves flattened, and soon after, the clicks from the speakers in her ears no longer elicited a response. As Sabom described, "Total brain shutdown."[64] She was connected to a heart-lung machine, which provides artificial circulation, in order to deliver blood to her body (but not to her brain). The head of the operating table was tilted up, and the blood was drained from Pam's head "like oil from a car."[65]

---

63. Sabom, *Light and Death*, 41.
64. Sabom, *Light and Death*, 43.
65. Sabom, *Light and Death*, 43.

Sometime during this procedure, Pam felt a presence, then saw a pinpoint of light, which pulled her into a tunnel. She began to discern figures and heard her grandmother calling. Pam recalled that sometime during this period she felt a sensation of being pulled quickly through a vortex that she described as being "like a tunnel but it wasn't a tunnel."[66]

> At some point very early in the tunnel vortex I became aware of my grandmother calling me. But I didn't hear her call me with my ears…It was a clearer hearing than with my ears. I trust the sense more than I trust my own ears. The feeling was that she wanted me to come to her, so I continued with no fear down the shaft. It's a dark shaft that I went through, and at the very end there was this very little tiny pinpoint of light that kept getting bigger and bigger and bigger.

Pam described how she entered the light, and once there, sensed presences that at first she could not see. Then she was able to discern different figures in the light, which slowly began to form shapes she could recognize. "And it felt *great*," as she exclaimed on the BBC documentary.

She saw many people she knew when they were alive on Earth, some she did not, and yet she felt connected to all of them.

> Everyone I saw, looking back on it, fit perfectly into my understanding of what that person looked like at their best during their lives.
>
> I recognized a lot of people. My uncle Gene was there. So was my great-great Aunt Maggie, who was really a cousin. On Papa's side of the family, my grandfather was there…They were specifically taking care of me, looking after me.

---

66. Sabom, *Light and Death*, 50.

They would permit me to go no further… It was communicated to me—that's the best way I know how to say it, because they didn't speak like I'm speaking—that if I went all the way into the light something would happen to me physically. They would be unable to put this me back into the body me, like I had gone too far and they couldn't reconnect. So they wouldn't let me go anywhere or do anything.

When all the blood had drained from Pam's brain, the aneurysm "collapsed like a deflated balloon."[67] It was removed by Spetzler, the cardiopulmonary machine was turned back on, and warm blood was pumped back into her body. But Pam's heart was still in cardiac arrest, due to the state of ventricular fibrillation, a form of disturbance that was caused by the induced hypothermia. No blood would have been pushed through to her brain because there would have been no squeezing action, only uncontrollable quivering. Electric shocks would be required to restart the normal rhythm of her heart.

On film, Pam described the close of her NDE:

At some point in time, I was reminded that it was time to go back. My uncle was the one who brought me back down to the body. But then I got to where the body was, and I looked at the thing, and I for sure did not want to get in it, because it looked pretty much like what it was, as in: void of life. And I knew it would hurt so I didn't want to get in. But he kept reasoning with me, he says: "Like diving into a swimming pool, just jump in." No. [laughs] "What about the children?" You know what? I think the children will be fine. [laughs] He pushed me; he gave me a little help there. I saw the body jump. I saw it do

---

67. Sabom, *Light and Death*, 45.

this number [lurches chest forward]. And then he pushed me, and I *felt* it do this number [lurches chest forward again].[68]

She recalled hearing the song "Hotel California" playing in the room and witnessing her body being shocked *twice* in order to restart her heart. Anywhere from one to multiple shocks may be needed to restart the heart. Rivas, Dirven, and Smit pointed out that "at that moment, with her heart stopped and the blood drained from her brain, there was with absolute certainty no brain activity anymore that could support conscious mental function."[69]

Neurosurgeon Karl Greene was involved in the operation, and in an interview said, "She knew her heart had to be stimulated twice to restart. She shouldn't have known that … She was physiologically dead. No brain wave activity, no heartbeat, nothing. No blood inside her body of any consequence. She was dead."[70]

Pam was interviewed on CBS's *48 Hours*, along with Dr. Spetzler. Spetzler left no doubt about Pam's clinical condition during hypothermic cardiac arrest: "If you would examine that patient from a clinical perspective during that hour, that patient by all definition would be dead. At this point there is no brain activity, no blood going through the brain. Nothing, nothing, nothing."[71]

Speaking with the wisdom and humility of a true scientist, Dr. Spetzler admitted:

I don't have an explanation for it. I don't know how it's possible for it to happen, considering the physiological state she was in. At the same time, I have seen so many things that I can't

68. Broome, 2002.
69. Rivas et al., *The Self Does Not Die*, 100.
70. Quoted in Rivas et al., 101.
71. Sabom, *Light and Death*, 50.

explain, that I don't want to be so arrogant as to be able to say that there is no way it can happen.[72]

Was Pam really dead?

Critics sometimes retort that NDEs do not provide evidence for survival, as the patients were not "really dead." What they always mean by this is that they think death means irreversibility. But this is to miss the point entirely. The point has nothing to do with a quibble over a dictionary definition.

Although the definition of clinical death differs somewhat from country to country, there are usually three criteria:

- No spontaneous breathing
- No heartbeat
- Fixed, dilated pupils, indicating no activity in the brain stem

By all three measures Pam's body was clinically dead. And yet she reported the deepest NDE ever reported, including clear cognitive function that provides all indication of occurring at a time when there was every medical reason to consider her brain as entirely nonfunctioning.

And as for whether or not Pam was "really dead," we can let Pam herself have the last word: "I think death is an illusion, a really nasty and bad lie."[73]

Ability of Separated Consciousness to Hear Sound

In 2011, militant skeptic Gerald Woerlee, whom we met earlier with regard to the Lloyd Rudy case, volunteered to submit a critique of the Pam Reynolds case to the *Journal of Near-Death Studies*, and I was asked to submit a rebuttal. Woerlee's arguments

---

72. Broome, *The Day I Died*.
73. Broome, *The Day I Died*.

centered around a metaphysical point he obviously considered impressive. He wrote:

> If a disembodied conscious mind can pass through several concrete floors without experiencing any apparent resistance, then it will certainly not interact in any way with the infinitely less solid air pressure variations of sound waves in air caused by speech or music. Accordingly, an apparently disembodied conscious mind is unable to hear sound waves in air.[74]

Note, however, that Reynolds commented that her vision "was not like normal vision. It was brighter and more focused and clearer than normal vision" and that her hearing "was a clearer hearing than with my ears." Clearer-than-normal hearing is not what one would normally expect a person to report from a time when their ears were covered with tape and gauze with 100 decibel clicks in one ear and white noise hissing into the other.

Anesthesiologist Stuart Hameroff also submitted a rebuttal in the same issue, and I agreed with Hameroff when he replied: "Auditory consciousness without ears (and visual consciousness without eyes) are not problematic, because the means by which auditory or visual consciousness occur with ears and eyes is unknown."[75]

His point, of course, is that researchers simply have no idea how electrical and chemical activity in the brain is transformed into the conscious experience of sense perception. We should consider the everyday phenomenon of sensory experience to be simply astounding, but because it is commonplace, we take it for granted. The fact that reported disembodied perception is relatively rare does not imply that reports of such perception should

---

74. Woerlee, "Could Pam Reynolds Hear?" 7.
75. Hameroff, "Response to 'Could Pam Reynolds Hear?'" 27.

be ruled out on the *a priori* grounds that it is mysterious, because embodied perception is *also* deeply mysterious.

Woerlee seems to be committing the fallacy of thinking that if we cannot explain *how* something occurs, then this means *that* it does not occur. We encountered this fallacy earlier, and noted how this fallacy appears repeatedly in the history of science. Reports of rocks that fall from the sky—what today are known as meteorites—were dismissed by scientists for decades on the grounds that there are no rocks in the sky to fall. For decades, geologists ridiculed Wegener's evidence for continental drift because he could offer no convincing explanation for how the landmasses moved about. And such antiempiricism can cause great suffering: consider that before bacteria and their role in disease were known, physicians rejected the practice of handwashing because it made no sense to them, despite evidence that the practice resulted in meaningful declines in hospital deaths.

So, at the present stage of scientific understanding, little more can be said other than that any disembodied perception of the surrounding environment is mediated via a different process than that of embodied perception. At the present, *what this process may be can only be speculated*.

Conclusion

Several features of the near-death experience seem to suggest survival:

1. Normal or enhanced mental processes at a time when brain processes are severely impaired or entirely absent.
2. Out-of-body view of one's own body, and of the surrounding environment.

3. Perception of deceased acquaintances.
4. Corroborated perception of events not accessible to one's biological sense organs, apparently while out of the body.

The first suggests that mental clarity is not entirely dependent on a properly functioning brain; the second that consciousness can function apart from the physical body; the third, that those who have died before us continue to exist; and the fourth, that these experiences are not entirely subjective.

But the main relevance of the NDE for our topic is the fact that it proves false the materialist idea that consciousness depends on a functioning brain.

Chapter 6
Deathbed Visions

Extraordinary visions experienced shortly before death have been reported throughout history, but the first systematic attempt to study the phenomenon was made by a physics professor at the Royal College of Science in Dublin, Sir William Barrett.

On the night of January 12, 1924, Barrett's wife, a physician, rushed home to tell her husband of a remarkable event she had witnessed. She had delivered the child of a woman named Doris, and although the baby was delivered safely, Doris herself lay dying. Lady Barrett described what happened next:

> Suddenly, she looked eagerly towards one part of the room, a radiant smile illuminating her whole countenance. "Oh, lovely, lovely," she said. I asked, "What is lovely?" "What I *see*," she replied in low intense tones. "What do you see?" "Lovely brightness—wonderful beings." It is difficult to describe the sense of reality conveyed by her intense absorption in the vision. Then—seeming to focus her attention more intently on one place for a moment—she exclaimed, almost with a kind of joyous cry, "Why, it's

Father! Oh, he's so glad I'm coming; he *is* so glad. It would be perfect if only W. (her husband) would come too."

Her baby was brought for her to see. She looked at it with interest, and then said, "Do you think I ought to stay for baby's sake?" Then turning towards the vision again, she said, "I can't—I can't stay; if you could see what I do, you would know I can't stay."

Yet suddenly, she was surprised to see her sister Vida also with her father. Vida had died three weeks previous, but Doris had not been told because of her precarious health.

She spoke to her father, saying, "I am coming," turning at the same time to look at me, saying, "Oh, he is so near." On looking at the same place again, she said with a rather puzzled expression, "He has Vida with him," turning again to me saying, "Vida is with him." Then she said, "You do want me, Dad; I am coming."[76]

Deeply impressed by his wife's report, Barrett collected this and other cases he could find into a small book entitled *Death Bed Visions*, published in 1926. Barrett concluded that deathbed visions tend to be of apparitions of the dead, who seem to the dying person to appear with the purpose of taking them away. When such visions occur, the dying person is usually rational and clear-minded, and the dying person often reacts with emotions of joy or serenity.

Thirty years later, Barrett's work inspired a modern large-scale study, undertaken by Karlis Osis and Erlendur Haraldsson, that surveyed thousands of physicians and nurses regarding their experiences with dying patients in both the United States and India. As with the earlier study, most visions were of otherworldly visitors, usually deceased relatives, which were reported by patients

---

76. Barrett, *Death Bed Visions*, 14.

as being there to take the dying person away. Osis and Haraldsson summarized their results:

> In both the United States and India, the visions of the dying and of near-death patients were overwhelmingly dominated by apparitions of the dead and religious figures. This finding is loud and clear: *When the dying see apparitions, they are nearly always experienced as messengers from a postmortem mode of existence.*[77]

Osis and Haraldsson considered various alternative explanations for such cases, including drugs, disease, and religious expectations; after rigorous statistical analysis, they rejected them all.

There are also several other cases on record of the patient claiming to see a friend or relative of whose recent death they were unaware.

The following case was reported by Dr. Minot Savage. It involves two American girls eight years of age—Jennie and Edith—who were close friends. In June of 1889 both caught diphtheria, and Jennie died at noon on a Wednesday. Edith's parents decided not to tell her that Jennie had died, and shortly before Edith died, she asked her parents to give Jennie two photographs and to say goodbye to Jennie for her. According to witnesses,

> She appeared to see … friends she knew were dead … But now suddenly, and with every appearance of surprise, she turned to her father and exclaimed, "Why Papa, I am going to take Jennie with me! Why Papa! You did not tell me that Jennie was here! And immediately she reached out her arms as if in welcome, and said, "Oh, Jennie, I'm so glad you are here!"[78]

---

77. Osis and Haraldsson, *At the Hour of Death*, 184. Emphasis in original.
78. Dr. Minot Savage, *Psychic Facts and Theories*. Cited in Currie, *You Cannot Die!*, 160.

A more modern case involving a person from a non-Western culture was reported by two nurses who have spent decades working with the dying. The case involved a dignified Chinese woman, Su, who was getting devoted care from her daughter, Lily. Both were Buddhists and very accepting of the mother's terminal status:

> "I've had a good life for ninety-three years," she said. "And I've been on this earth long enough!" She dreamed often of her husband, who had died some years before.
>
> "I will join him soon," she said.
>
> But one day Su seemed very puzzled.
>
> "Why is my sister with my husband?" she asked. "They are both calling me to come."
>
> "Is your sister dead?" I asked.
>
> "No, she still lives in China," she said. "I have not seen her for many years."
>
> When I related this conversation to the daughter, she was astonished and tearful.
>
> "My aunt died two days ago in China," Lily said. "We decided not to tell Mother—her sister had the same kind of cancer. It was a very painful death; she lived in a remote village where good medical care wasn't available. We didn't want to upset or frighten Mother, since she is so sick herself."[79]

When the mother was told of her sister's illness and death, she smiled and said, "Now I understand." She died three weeks later, at peace.

Another modern case was described by Natalie Kalmus, a pioneer developer of the technicolor process. Natalie's sister Eleanor was dying, with Natalie beside her at the last moments of her life:

> I sat on her bed and took her hand. It was on fire. Then Eleanor seemed to rise up in bed, almost to a sitting position.

---

79. Callanan and Kelley, 1992, 93–4.

"Natalie," she said, "there are so many of them. There's Fred and Ruth—what's she doing here?"

An electric shock went through me. She had said Ruth! Ruth was her cousin, who had died suddenly the week before. But I knew that Eleanor had not been told of the sudden death ... I felt on the verge of some wonderful, almost frightening knowledge ...

Her voice was surprisingly clear. "It's so confusing. There are so many of them!" Suddenly her arms stretched out happily. "I am going up," she murmured.[80]

Shortly after, Eleanor died.

These cases were considered in my second book. As for an explanation in terms of ESP, I concluded:

The skeptic must say that the dying person telepathically or clairvoyantly gains true information about a recently deceased friend or relative, but about nothing else; and that the rest of the content of the vision is pure hallucination. It should be clear that this is a purely *ad hoc* theory, invented to explain these cases and nothing else. If this theory is to be more than merely dogma, it must be independently testable. And if this theory is to be testable, then from it certain predictions must follow. But there is not a shred of independent evidence that the dying become more clairvoyant or telepathic in the final moments of life; and not a shred of independent evidence that ESP "dresses up" knowledge of unpleasant occurrences into pleasant hallucinations. The predictions of the theory *in its testable form* are not borne out; and if the theory is still maintained, then it is just another example of what Popper called an "immunizing tactic."[81]

---

80. R. DeWitt Miller, *You DO Take it With You*. Cited in Currie, *You Cannot Die!*, 161.

81. Carter, *Science and the Near-Death Experience*, 267.

Chapter 7
Apparitions

Accounts of apparitions of the deceased come from virtually all societies of which we have record. Stories conveyed as fact come from ancient Greece and Rome, and Saint Augustine wrote about them as familiar occurrences. The following is an account presented as genuine from classical literature.

As told by Pliny the Younger, the philosopher Athenodorus one day heard that a house was going cheaply in Athens because it was haunted by the specter of an old man, described as skinny and dirty, with fetters on his legs and clanking chains on his wrists. Considering the house a curious bargain, the philosopher decided to rent it. On the first night, as he sat reading a book, he first heard the chains, and then he saw the figure. It beckoned him into the garden, and the philosopher followed. After pointing to a spot on the ground, the specter suddenly vanished. Athenodorus marked the spot with some grass and leaves, and on the next day had the local magistrates dig there. A skeleton in chains was found and given a proper burial. From that time on, we are told, the haunting ceased.[82]

---

82. Inglis, *Natural and Supernatural*, 186.

Modern reports of apparitions are surprisingly common: in an Icelandic survey, Haraldsson reported "that 14 percent of our original representative national sample may have experienced visual apparitions of the dead."[83] John Palmer surveyed the residents of Charlottesville, Virginia, and found that 7.5 percent of 622 respondents claimed to have had the visual impression of an apparition.[84]

In appearance, apparitions are typically described as looking like a normal person, so much so that they are typically mistaken for living persons. They may cast a shadow and be reflected in a mirror. If more than one person sees the apparition, then each person will see the apparition from the proper perspective. However, in other respects, apparitions do not resemble living persons: they may appear and disappear in locked rooms, vanish while being watched, or pass through physical objects.

A prominent characteristic of apparitions of the dead is the high frequency of persons who died violently. Haraldsson found that 30 percent of his Icelandic cases involved encounters with persons who had died violently, almost identical to the 28 percent frequency of violent death found among the nineteenth century British cases of *Phantasms of the Living*.[85]

Collectively Perceived Apparitions

There have been many accounts of the same apparition perceived by more than one person, at the same time, or at different times. Although most sightings of apparitions have been by those who were alone at the time, there has been no shortage of reports of collectively perceived apparitions. Frederic Myers, one of the founding members of the British Society for Psychical Research,

83. Haraldsson, "Survey of Claimed Encounters with the Dead," 106.

84. Stevenson, "The Contribution of Apparitions to the Evidence for Survival," 345.

85. Stevenson, "The Contribution of Apparitions to the Evidence for Survival," 346.

wrote that when two or more persons are present at the time an apparition is perceived, in two-thirds of such cases two or more persons perceive it.[86]

The Cheltenham Ghost

The following is perhaps the most famous and well-researched of all haunting cases. It is also considered one of the most convincing of the well over one hundred cases of collectively perceived apparitions recorded by the British Society for Psychical Research. The Cheltenham ghost was frequently seen by at least seventeen people, and heard by more than twenty. Always described as a tall woman dressed in black, she was sometimes seen by two or more people at the same time, or, more frequently, by different people at different times, including sightings by people who had not heard of any ghostly visitor. Dogs also reacted to her presence, usually with terror.

This case concerns the haunting of a large stone house in Cheltenham, England. The apparition first appeared in 1882 to Rosina Despard, then a nineteen-year-old medical student living at home with her family. The earliest accounts of the haunting were written under the pseudonym of Miss R. C. Morton, and it was not until years later that the family name and location of the home were made public. Rosina did not wish to jeopardize her medical career—unusual for a woman at the time—and her father feared for the value of the property.

In her written account, Rosina described that one night after she had retired to her room, she heard someone outside her door. Upon opening the door, she at first saw no one, but after stepping into the hallway, she saw the figure of a tall lady dressed in black,

---

86. As reported in Stevenson, "The Contribution of Apparitions to the Evidence for Survival," 349.

standing at the top of the stairs. After a few moments, the figure descended the stairs, and Rosina followed. However, the small piece of candle she was holding went out, and she returned to her room. She wrote:

> The figure was that of a tall lady, dressed in black of a soft woolen material, judging from the slight sound in moving. The face was hidden in a handkerchief held in the right hand. This was all I noticed then; but on further occasions, when I was able to observe her more closely, I saw the upper part of the left side of the forehead, and a little of the hair above. Her left hand was nearly hidden by her sleeve and a fold of her dress. As she held it down a portion of a widow's cuff was visible on both wrists, so that the whole impression was that of a lady in widow's weeds.[87]

During the next two years Rosina saw the figure about half a dozen times, and did not mention her experiences to other family members or servants. During this period, it was seen on three occasions by others. First her sister saw a tall figure in black enter the drawing room, and asked others, "Who was that Sister of Mercy whom I have just seen going into the drawing room?" She was told there was no such visitor, and after checking the drawing room, found that it was empty. She wrote, "This was the year before I heard of any appearance being known of in the house."[88] Next, a housemaid reported seeing the figure, and apparently thought that an intruder had entered the house. Finally, Rosina's younger brother and a friend, then eight or nine, while playing outside "both saw a tall figure in black holding a handkerchief to her face with her right hand, seated at the writing table in the

---

87. Morton, "Record of a Haunted House," 313.
88. Morton, "Record of a Haunted House," 326.

window, and therefore in full light." The boys ran in to see who the visitor was, but found no one. Her brother later signed a statement that "it was full daylight at the time," and that prior to this sighting, "I had heard nothing about anything unusual being seen in the house."[89] After this, Rosina told the rest of the family that she had seen the figure several times in the past two years.

Rosina attempted several times to speak to the figure, but received no reply, only once "a slight gasp." She glued strings across the staircase, through which the figure simply passed. Attempts to touch the apparition were also unsuccessful.

On the evening of August 11, 1884, Rosina and her sister both saw the apparition standing on the balcony, looking into the window for several minutes. The following evening, Rosina spotted the figure outside and watched her enter an open side door. Later that same evening, one of her younger sisters was alone in the drawing room singing when she felt a cold shiver and saw the apparition bend over her as if to turn the pages of her songbook. Another sister came in from the garden, saying that she saw the figure outside. The sisters mounted a search, and Rosina's older sister called out from a window that she saw the figure outside, walking toward the orchard. On that evening, four people reported seeing the apparition.

According to the reports, animals also reacted to the apparition. A large retriever who slept in the kitchen was on several occasions found by the cook in a state of terror in the morning. Rosina insisted that the dog "was kindly treated and not at all a nervous dog." She also described the reactions of a small terrier:

Twice, I remember seeing this dog suddenly run up to the mat at the foot of the stairs, wagging its tail, and moving its back

89. Morton, "Record of a Haunted House," 326.

in the way dogs do when expecting to be caressed. It jumped up, fawning as it would do if a person had been standing there, but suddenly slunk away with its tail between its legs, and retreated, trembling, under a sofa. We were all under the impression that it had seen the figure.[90]

Who could she have been? The family launched an investigation and concluded the most likely candidate was Imogen Swinhoe, second wife of Henry Swinhoe, the house's first occupant in 1860. According to those who had known her, Imogen bore a strong resemblance to descriptions of the figure. Sadly, the marriage does not seem to have been a happy one, and Mrs. Swinhoe left her husband. She went to Bristol, where she died in 1878, at the age of forty-one.

The British Society for Psychical Research first heard about the case several years after it had apparently begun, but were not about to simply accept Rosina's account without corroboration. Frederic Myers, whom we met earlier, was dispatched to join the investigation in 1885, and he promptly interviewed all the principal witnesses and obtained several written accounts from them. Of the various accounts, he wrote: "In this case it is observable that the phenomena as seen or heard by all the witnesses were very uniform in character—even in the numerous instances where there had been no previous communication between the percipients." With the exception of one incident an elderly man could not recall six years later, he "found no discrepancy in the independent testimonies."[91]

Could it have all been an elaborate hoax? Myers could find not one shred of evidence that Rosina had either fabricated or

90. Morton, "Record of a Haunted House," 323.
91. Morton, "Record of a Haunted House," 311.

reported the events inaccurately. And it is hard to conceive of a possible motive for such a hoax. As mentioned earlier, the original report was written under the pseudonym R. C. Morton because of several legitimate concerns: Rosina feared that exposure may jeopardize her medical career, and Captain Despard feared for the market value of the house. The family also apparently tried to keep the apparition a secret because of the difficulty reports of it caused in attracting and retaining servants.

A Father's Visit

The following dramatic case also involves a collectively perceived apparition.

On Christmas Eve, 1869, Mr. and Mrs. P., along with their fifteen-month-old daughter, had just settled in for the night. As usual, the couple had carefully locked all the doors, including the door to their bedroom. Mrs. P. had asked her husband to leave a lamp burning in the bedroom before he got into bed so that Mrs. P. could feed her daughter. The lamp, sitting on a set of drawers at the other end of the room, had been turned down so that the room was dimly lit. Mrs. P. described what happened next.

> I [was] just pulling myself into a half-sitting posture against the pillows, thinking of nothing but the arrangements for the following day, when to my great astonishment I saw a gentleman standing at the foot of the bed, dressed as a naval officer, and with a cap on his head having a projecting peak. The light being in the position which I have indicated, the face was in shadow *to me*, and the more so that the visitor was leaning upon his arms which rested on the foot-rail of the bedstead. I was too astonished to be afraid, but simply wondered who it could be; and instantly touching my husband's shoulder (whose face was turned from me), I said, "Willie, who is this?" My husband

turned, and for a second or two lay looking in intense astonishment at the intruder; then lifting himself a little, he shouted
"What on earth are you doing here, sir?" Meanwhile the form,
slowly drawing himself into an upright position, now said in a
commanding, yet reproachful voice, "Willie! Willie!"

I looked at my husband and saw that his face was white
and agitated. As I turned towards him he sprang out of bed
as though to attack the man, but stood by the bedside as if
afraid, or in great perplexity, while the figure calmly and slowly
moved towards the wall at right angles with the lamp. As it
passed the lamp, a deep shadow fell upon the room as of a
material person shutting out the light from us by his interven-
ing body, and he disappeared, as it were, into the wall. My husband now, in a very agitated manner, caught up the lamp, and
turning to me said, "I mean to look all over the house, and see
where he is gone." … without pausing, my husband *unlocked
the door*, hastened out of the room, and was soon searching the
whole house.[92]

While her husband searched the house, Mrs. P. sat in bed, convinced that they had seen an apparition, and wondering what it
could possibly mean. Her brother Arthur was in the navy, and she
wondered if this meant he was somehow in trouble. After her
husband returned from his fruitless search, she expressed her fear
that the apparition had something to do with Arthur, to which he
replied, "Oh! No, it was my father!"

My husband's father *had been dead fourteen years*: he had been a
naval officer in his young life; but, through ill-health, had left
the service before my husband was born, and the latter had
only once or twice seen him in uniform. I had never seen him
at all. My husband and I related the occurrence to my uncle

---

92. Myers, "On Recognized Apparitions Occurring More Than a Year after Death," 27–28.

and aunt, and we all noticed that my husband's agitation and anxiety were very great: whereas his usual manner was calm and reserved in the extreme, and he was a thorough and avowed sceptic in all so-called supernatural events.[93]

Later, her husband confessed to her that he had been about to take the advice of a man who almost certainly would have led him into ruin. Only the apparition of his dead father had stopped him from following this course.

Mrs. P. continued:

As the weeks passed, my husband gradually disclosed to me that he had been in great financial difficulties; and that, at the time his father was thus sent to us, he was inclining to take the advice of a man who would certainly—had my husband yielded to him (as he had intended before hearing the warning voice)—have led him to ruin, perhaps worse. It is this fact which makes us most reticent in speaking of the event; in addition to which, my husband had already been led to speculate upon certain chances which resulted in failure, and infinite sorrow to both of us as well as to others.

None of us were particularly ready to believe in such evidences, so that no condition of "over-wrought nerves," or "superstitious fears," could have been the cause of the manifestation.

Mrs. P. concluded that the apparition was "a direct warning to my husband in the voice and appearance of the one that he had most revered in all his life, and was the most likely to obey."[94]

Mrs. P.'s account was corroborated in writing by her husband, and another couple acknowledged that Mrs. P. had told them the same story years earlier. Myers wrote:

93. Myers, "On Recognized Apparitions Occurring More Than a Year after Death," 28.
94. Myers, "On Recognized Apparitions Occurring More Than a Year after Death," 28–29.

Mr. P. confirms as follows, June 17, 1885:

> Without wishing to add more to the incidents recorded
> herein by my wife, I would simply note that the details
> are quite correct, and that the occurrence took place as
> stated. W. B. P.

Dr. and Mrs. C, friends of Mrs. and Mr. P., add the following
note:

> June 16th, 1885
> This narrative was told us by Mrs. P., as here recorded,
> some years ago.
> J. C. Ellen H. C.[95]

Could these three signed reports have all been part of a hoax?
Myers could find not one shred of evidence that Mrs. P. had
reported the events inaccurately. And it is hard to conceive of a
possible motive for such a hoax. The original reports were written
under the pseudonyms "Mr. and Mrs. P." obviously to avoid the
embarrassment of Mr. P.'s actual and intended financial acts ("It is
this fact which makes us most reticent in speaking of the event").
Also, recall Mrs. P.'s description of her husband as "a thorough
and avowed sceptic in all so-called supernatural events."

Animals Share the Experience

The following case is very odd: it concerns an apparition that is
unknown to the witness, and is also apparently perceived by two
dogs. This account was related to the American Society for Psychical Research (ASPR) by an officer in the US navy. After being been
assigned to the Naval Powder Factory at Indian Head, Maryland,
in 1926, the officer, his wife, and their two dogs, moved into one

---

95. Myers, "On Recognized Apparitions Occurring More Than a Year after Death," 29.

half of a double house. In September 1927, another officer and his family moved into the other half, and the two families became close friends. In his letter to the ASPR, the lieutenant writes:

> Early in the following March, I was sitting at a card table in the den, solving a problem in navigation. I was facing the front of the house. The time was about 12:25 a.m. Both dogs were sleeping on the floor at the end of a davenport in the living room. I heard the spaniel growl; but as he often growls at the marine sentry as he passes the house, I paid no attention to it. Both dogs then got up, passed me in the den and went down the back hall into the dining-room where both dogs again growled and then tore madly across the hall and up the stairway. The noise they made going up the stairs awakened my wife, who was asleep on the second floor.
>
> Surprised at their actions, I looked up from my work and saw a man standing in the living room near the hall archway. He was probably twenty-two feet from me. All outside doors and windows were closed … I could see him plainly.[96]

The duties of the lieutenant meant that it was not uncommon for men to come to the house at all hours. However, the lieutenant was surprised that the man could have entered without his hearing the doors open and close, and the lieutenant was irritated that the man did not knock or ring the doorbell. He also did not recognize the man as an employee of the factory. The officer stared at the man for about ten seconds, as the stranger seemed about to speak. Then, he rose from his chair and took a few steps forward to greet the man, and the stranger vanished instantly.

After a careful search of the house assured the lieutenant that all the doors and windows were closed, the lieutenant concluded that he had been seeing things after working too long, and turned

96. Lieut. A. M. H., "An Apparition Identified from a Photograph," 54.

in for the night. His wife, who had been awakened by the mad dash of the dogs up the stairs, he told nothing of his experience.

However, about a week later, when he was alone in the house at about 9:00 p.m., the lieutenant again saw the man standing in the living room, in excellent light.

> As I entered the den from the back hall, I saw the same man standing in about the center of the living room. This distance was about twenty feet, not more than that. The light was excellent and I could see his features plainly. I was not in the least frightened. Again he seemed about to speak, and again I waited—this time probably fifteen minutes. I took about two full steps towards him, which brought me within fifteen or sixteen feet of him at the most, when, again, *he wasn't there!*

The man appeared to weigh a little over two hundred pounds, was dressed in light gray clothing, looked like he had a deep tan, and gave every appearance of being solid.

About ten minutes later, the lieutenant visited his neighbor in the other part of the house to get his opinion. When the neighbor's wife came into the room, her husband told him that the lieutenant had seen a ghost that he did not recognize. At this point the woman put about twenty photographs before the lieutenant and asked him to look through them.

> I shuffled then through carelessly and at about the seventh or eighth picture I came across the portrait of the man I had seen a few minutes before. There is no doubt in my mind as to its being the same man. I would know him among a thousand.
>
> Dumbfounded, I said "That is the man. Who is he?" She replied "My father: he has been dead for several years."[97]

---

97. Lieut. A. M. H., "An Apparition Identified from a Photograph," 55.

About ten days later, he saw the same man again, standing in the main hallway near the front door. After getting within ten feet, the man again simply vanished. About ten days after this, the lieutenant saw the man for the final time in the back hallway leading to the kitchen. Three lights were burning in the kitchen, and the form of the man blocked the lights. When he disappeared after a few seconds, the lieutenant again could see the kitchen lights.

The lieutenant concluded his letter to the American Society of Psychical Research with these words:

> I am willing to swear to the truth of the above statement. I hope there is some simple explanation of all this, as I would hate to have my life-long faith in a ghostless world shattered. My parents taught me from childhood that ghosts did not and could not exist, and all my life I have firmly believed that to be true. Naturally the beliefs of a lifetime are hard to shatter. Hence this letter seeking an explanation of that which to me is inexplicable.[98]
>   Very respectfully,
>   A. M. H.
>   (Lieut. U.S.N.)

Could this case have been part of a hoax? It is difficult to see why a career officer in the US Navy would risk his career by making up such a story, which if false, could easily have been contradicted by the officer and wife living next door. On the contrary, the stated motive of the officer for relating his experience to the ASPR was the hope of finding an explanation *not* involving ghosts.

---

98. Lieut. A. M. H., "An Apparition Identified from a Photograph," 56.

Apparitions with Their Own Agenda

There are also reports of apparitions seeming to display a purpose that is all their own.

The Blue Orchid Case

Arthur C. Clarke, author of *2001: A Space Odyssey*, was told the following strange tale by Englishwoman Georgina Feakes:

Before the Second World War, Georgina's aunt Beatrice and her family had emigrated to South Africa. When hostilities broke out, Georgina's cousin Owen Howerson signed up and was killed in action in 1944. Soon after, Georgina claimed, he appeared to her in England, surrounded by a golden mist. "He said his tank had been hit, but he still felt very much alive. Would I please tell his mum, and please give his love to poor Helen." Georgina claims to have been dumbstruck at first. "I tried to speak, although my lips were numb and frozen." Finally, she says she found her voice: "I said 'Proof, give me proof.' And he said 'watch.'"

> To my amazement, he opened the top of his shirt, and took out a beautiful blue flower, of penetrating perfume. It was very beautiful, long and bell-like, orchid-like. A wonderful scent permeated the whole room. While I stared in amazement, he put it back in his shirt, took it out, and put it back, and took it out. And then he said, quite loudly, "tell mum, Table Mountain."

According to Georgina, the apparition then shimmered and vanished. With none of this making any sense to Georgina, she wrote at once to Owen's mother, and back from South Africa came this curious explanation. Owen had one day gone up Table Mountain, picked a protected blue flower, and brought it home, hidden in his shirt. The flower was a rare blue orchid that grew on Table

Mountain, and since it was illegal to pick, Owen had risked prison to bring it back to her. While showing it to her, the door slammed, and he nervously hid the flower in his shirt, only taking it out again after learning it was a false alarm. Her aunt Beatrice in South Africa had kept the story secret in order to protect Owen, who could have been imprisoned for the offence. So, it does not seem likely that Georgina could have known about the incident.

Georgina claims Owen appeared a second time, again in a golden mist. But this time his manner was not friendly. "He reproached me bitterly for not contacting Helen. And I was very distressed about this, because I had tried." His mother had been through all his correspondence, and had found no letter from anyone named Helen, or any reference to anyone with that name.

But there *had* been a Helen in Owen's life, a lovely young woman with dark hair and eyes for whom Owen had written romantic letters and poems. After reading the story of the blue orchid in the newspapers, she contacted the family, and the mystery of Helen was solved.[99]

Could this report simply be part of a hoax? As with the other cases above, it is difficult to imagine a possible motive. Picking the blue orchid was strictly illegal, and even though Owen was no longer among the living, the public report of such an act may have been a minor embarrassment to the family. Also, the whole story could easily have been refuted by Owen's mother, or by Helen. And if the family *had* known about Helen, then surely they would not have resorted to such a strange and roundabout method of contacting her.

On the other hand, although it is difficult to attribute a motive for a hoax to anyone living, a romantic motive for the appearance

---

99. Clarke, "World of Strange Powers: Messages from the Dead," described in Carter, *Science and the Afterlife*, 115–6.

and communication could easily be attributed to Owen if he still lived.

Alternative Explanations
Faulty Eyewitness Testimony

Reports of apparitions have frequently been criticized by materialist-skeptics on the grounds that it is possible they are the products of faulty eyewitness testimony.

For instance, Henry Gordon, magician, newspaper columnist, and member of the Committee for the Scientific Investigation of Claims of the Paranormal (CSICOP), briefly reviewed the work of sociologist Ian Currie on apparitions, and wrote:

> I find one basic weakness in Currie's arguments: His "evidence" is based on personal anecdotes and eyewitness testimony. To accept such evidence you have to agree that most people are reliable witnesses, that they have perfect memories, that they can trust the evidence of their senses. It's an illusion to believe this. There have been a great number of psychological studies done in the past few years on the subject of eyewitness testimony. It is flimsy. It is often unreliable. Apart from what these studies have revealed, it is also well known that eyewitness testimony has caused tragic errors to be made in some court cases.[100]

We have dealt with this general criticism earlier, and you will recall that a detailed investigation of a real-life criminal case found that the eyewitness testimony was in fact highly reliable, with the researchers concluding that "most of the witnesses in this case were highly accurate in their accounts, and this continued to be true 5 months after the event."

---

100. Gordon, *Extrasensory Deception*, 103.

The fact that eyewitness testimony is *sometimes* flawed does not imply that it is *always* flawed. Each individual case must be considered separately and on its own merits, and once a *prima facie* argument has been made for the validity of a specific instance of eyewitness testimony, then the burden of proof is on the critic to provide evidence that *in this particular case* there is reason to question the validity of the eyewitness accounts.

In other words, the wholesale dismissal of all reports of apparitions based simply upon the fact that eyewitness testimony is *sometimes* flawed raises the burden of proof from beyond all reasonable doubt to beyond all conceivable doubt, an impossible standard to meet when dealing with factual matters.

This is similar to a criminal case in which the prosecution has presented a consistent core of testimony from several independent eyewitnesses who have no apparent reason to lie, who have good reputations, good eyesight, good memories, and seem to have had a clear view of the incident. Such eyewitness testimony provides a strong *prima facie* argument, and the burden of proof then rests with the defense to present reasons why *in this particular case* the eyewitness testimony cannot be trusted. If during closing arguments the defense attorney responded by simply declaring, "We know that eyewitness testimony is sometimes flawed, so it is *possible* [in a logical sense] that this eyewitness testimony is also flawed," then this would obviously be an attempt to raise the standard of proof from beyond all reasonable doubt to beyond all *conceivable* doubt (unfortunately, an all-too-common tactic among both "skeptics" and criminal defense lawyers).

And what *of* the specific cases mentioned above? The Cheltenham ghost was first described by an educated and highly intelligent member of a respected family, and she claimed to have seen it on a number of occasions. It was also reportedly seen by at least seventeen people, often in good light, occasionally at the same time, over a period of years. The descriptions of the apparitions were consistent, and there appears to be no motive at all for lying or exaggeration—quite the opposite, as the family made efforts to avoid publicity. In the second case, the wife's testimony of her father-in-law's visit was corroborated in writing by her husband and by two friends of the family. This report also seems to lack any motive for lying. And what reason is there to suppose that the written testimony of a highly skeptical naval officer—that on four separate occasions he witnessed the apparition of a man in his quarters to which his dogs reacted—is "flimsy" or "unreliable"?

The burden of proof should properly be placed on "skeptics" such as Gordon to provide *specific* reasons why the testimony of the witnesses in each one of the cases above should be considered flawed.

Hallucination

But Gordon does not dismiss all accounts of apparitions only on grounds of possible mistaken eyewitness testimony. He thinks that many people who have reported seeing apparitions may have had a genuine experience—of sorts. Gordon writes that "the most common psychological explanation for seeing ghosts is that of hallucination." And in cases in which more than one person reported seeing the apparition, Gordon asserts that "the power of suggestion is the explanation."[101]

But when we consider specific cases, does this explanation make any sense? Consider the Cheltenham ghost: the hallucination theory fails to account for instances in which other people saw the apparition before Rosina reported her experiences. It also

---

101. Gordon, *Extrasensory Deception*, 103–4. Emphasis added.

fails to account for sightings reported by maids who, for obvious reasons, had not been told about the ghost. It seems pointless to invoke the power of suggestion if nothing has been suggested.

In the second case, we must hypothesize that the wife hallucinated the figure of a man she did not recognize, but who was later recognized as her husband's father, but only after he shared in the hallucination. In the third case, are we really prepared to believe that a naval officer hallucinated—on four separate occasions—the appearance of a man he did not know, and whom he later recognized as the father of a next-door neighbor? Finally, in the case of the blue orchid, the so-called hallucination revealed three facts that were later corroborated and acted with a purpose that was only that of the deceased person being supposedly hallucinated.

And these are not the only difficulties with the hallucination theory. We have also seen cases in which more than one person reports seeing an apparition at the same time.

Here Gordon also has a ready answer: "The fact is, once again, that *studies have shown that collective hallucinations do take place.* And the power of suggestion is the explanation."[102]

What studies? Gordon provides no references. As research, I combed through the entire *PsychInfo* database from 1887 to the time of writing and could find only *one* article on collective hallucinations. It appeared in the *Royal Naval Medical Service Journal* in 1942, and it described the experiences of the shipwrecked survivors of a torpedoed ship in Arctic waters. Out of the hundreds of men who managed to make it to rafts and lifeboats, only thirty-six survived, and two of these died shortly after being rescued. The men were without food and water for three days before help arrived.

---

102. Gordon, *Extrasensory Deception*, 103–4. Emphasis added.

The mortality rate was so high, and the exhaustion of the men so great, that they were finally unable to jettison the dead.

The shipwrecked survivors told a horrific tale of hunger, thirst, bitter cold, and despair. By the third day, some of the men in the floats started to hallucinate. They claimed to see land, a dockyard, and ships on the horizon. Although some of the other men remained skeptical, others began to think they also saw these things. Most of the visions were seen on the horizon, at what seemed a distance of several miles, and no humans were seen. Most of the visions only lasted a few minutes, although some seemed to have lasted an hour or so. After each vision ceased, most of the men realized what they had seen was only an illusion, and their depression returned.

I found absolutely nothing in this single study that is in any way relevant to the vast majority of reports of apparitions. The author of the study, Surgeon Lieutenant-Commander E. W. Anderson, would almost certainly have agreed: he wrote that "it is hardly necessary to state that visual hallucinations in a setting of clear consciousness are rare, if indeed they ever occur. It is certain that in some of the cases described here consciousness was not always clear, and in some cases the subject was actually delirious."[103]

Anderson briefly mentions psychical research and quickly adds that "the observations here contain little relevant to this discussion."[104] Indeed, it seems preposterous to argue that the hallucinations experienced by these desperate and miserable men—which seemed to spread to some of those around them by the power of suggestion—could throw any light whatsoever upon most reports of collectively perceived apparitions.

---

103. Anderson, "Abnormal Mental States in Survivors, with Special Reference to Collective Hallucinations," 369.
104. Anderson, "Abnormal Mental States," 375.

In fact, the simple skeptical objections that reports of apparitions are due to faulty memory or hallucinations are the easiest to deal with. Back in 1886, Gurney, Myers, and Podmore, in their landmark book *Phantasms of the Living*, presented in great detail over seven hundred reports of apparitions. The three researchers tried very hard to exclude any cases that might be due to mistaken eyewitness identity, faulty memories, or fraud. They argued that *their cases must be explained away in detail*, and went on to describe the sheer number of improbable hypotheses that must be advanced if the best-documented cases are to be explained away.

> We must make suppositions as detailed as the evidence itself. We must suppose that some people have a way of dating their letters in indifference to the calendar, or making entries in their diaries on the wrong page and never discovering their error; that when [a man] says that he is not subject to hallucinations of vision, it is through momentary forgetfulness of the fact that he has a spectral illusion once a week; that when a wife interrupts a husband's slumbers with words of distress or alarm, it is only her fun, or a sudden morbid craving for undeserved sympathy; and when people assert that they were in good health, in good spirits, and wide awake, at a particular time which they had occasion to note, it is a safe conclusion that they were having a nightmare, or were the prostrate victims of nervous hypochondria. Every one of these improbabilities is, perhaps, a possibility; but as the narratives drive us from one desperate expedient to another, and [we] see what is involved in the supposition that hundreds of persons of established character, known to us for the most part and unknown to one another, have simultaneously formed a plot to deceive us—there comes a point where the reason rebels.[105]

---

105. As quoted in Lorimer, *Survival?*, 182.

Super-ESP

Having eliminated fraud, faulty eyewitness testimony, and hallucination as explanations for the four cases above, we may think
that the skeptic has nothing left. But materialist-skeptics are not
the only type of skeptic. There are also those who have attempted
to explain reports of apparitions as due to remarkable powers of
telepathy, clairvoyance, or psychokinesis among the living.

However, the vast majority of experiencers do not have *any*
history of displaying remarkable powers of ESP or psychokinesis, and so it seems *ad hoc* in the extreme to speculate that these
individuals suddenly and temporarily acquired such remarkable
powers, in many cases equal to if not exceeding the powers of the
most remarkable subjects both inside and outside of the laboratory. It becomes even more *ad hoc* when we realize that outside
the laboratory the most remarkable mediums in history have typically been deep in trance when they perform, unlike the state of
the typical experiencer of an apparition.

At any rate, it is both unfair and lazy to dismiss all reports of
apparitions with the purely logical possibility that they may all
be explained as due to the sudden and temporary appearance of
powers of extrasensory perception far exceeding that found in any
laboratory or in any anecdotal report. As mentioned above, each
individual case needs be considered separately, and on its own
merits.

Consider the first case: at least seventeen people reported seeing the apparition. Did they all independently use extrasensory
perception to acquire information on the appearance of Imogen, a
woman they did not know ever lived? And then turn this information into a vision? For what purpose? Did the dogs in the house-

hold also do the same, even though they seemed terrified of the apparition?

If we attempt to explain the second case as a telepathically shared hallucination, we would first have to suppose that Mr. P. had been brooding or dreaming about what his long-dead father would have thought about his financial difficulties. Then we would have to suppose that Mrs. P. read her husband's mind, and then constructed a realistic hallucination of her husband's late father standing at the foot of the bed. After her husband was roused, he then telepathically picked up her vision, and also began hallucinating. The purpose of the figure—to stop the actions of Mr. P.—was actually Mr. P.'s own. He knew that what he was about to do was dangerous and wrong, but he needed to hallucinate a vision of his dead father to stop himself.

Can the third case involving the dogs be explained in terms of a telepathic hallucination? We would have to suppose that Mrs. G. was thinking of her late father, that the lieutenant telepathically read those thoughts and then created the hallucination of her father. Needless to say, this would be telepathy of an astonishing degree, exercised by a person who never before had any similar experience. What about the behavior of the dogs? They became excited immediately *before* the lieutenant first saw the figure, and so could not have been merely reacting to his astonishment. Are we to say that the dogs also telepathically read Mrs. G.'s thoughts at the same moment, and also began hallucinating? Finally, what possible motive could the lieutenant—or the dogs for that matter—have for telepathically acquiring information about a deceased man he had never met?

The Blue Orchid Case is also very difficult to explain in terms of telepathy among the living. If the purpose of the vision was to provide comfort for Helen, then it is difficult to understand why a vision of Owen should appear to someone who not only did not know that Owen was dead, but also did not know that he had a girlfriend named Helen. Also difficult to explain is the curious display of hiding a blue orchid in the shirt of the apparition, and the words *tell mum, Table Mountain*, all of which only made sense as the revelation of a secret crime after Owen's mother had been contacted. I do not know of a single case of telepathy or clairvoyance in which such detailed information is provided. Even more serious, I do not know of a single clear-cut case of telepathy or clairvoyance among the living in which the information is presented by a vision of another person, living or imaginary. Finally, examples of telepathy or clairvoyance among the living indicate that extrasensory perception is goal oriented—that is, used to fulfill a purpose that is obviously that of a living person or persons. However, in this case, information was provided in the form of a vision of a deceased person not known to be deceased, in terms of fulfilling a purpose difficult to attribute to the person who experienced the vision, yet in terms of fulfilling a purpose easily attributed to the deceased person, if they still lived.

Alan Gauld, commenting on these sorts of explanations, has written that "it cannot be denied that the Super-ESP theory's account of these cases is *ad hoc* and convoluted to the last degree. In fact, a flat-earther in full cry could hardly support his hypothesis with more tortuous argumentation, or with proposals less open to direct tests."[106] Gauld believes it is much simpler to suppose that discarnate agencies shape the collective experiences in accordance with their own purposes:

That way we can avoid such bizarre notions as that persons hitherto not known to be psychically gifted can suddenly

106. Gauld, *Mediumship and Survival*, 235.

develop powers of ESP comparable to, if not exceeding, the most remarkable that have ever been experimentally demonstrated; that two people without any conscious thought of doing any such thing can at an unconscious level telepathically link up with each other and hammer out the details of an hallucinatory figure which both shall see; that animals may to some extent share in this process; that the information thus acquired will be dressed up by processes unknown and presumably unconscious and presented to the conscious mind quite indirectly in the form of dramatic but really irrelevant interventions by deceased persons; and that the purposes promoted by the hallucinatory episodes, even when ostensibly more appropriate to the supposed deceased person, are really those of the living percipient or of some other living person whose mind telepathically influences his.[107]

---

107. Gauld, *Mediumship and Survival*, 235–6.

Chapter 8

Children Who Remember Previous Lives

Reincarnation is an ancient belief found in many diverse parts of the world. In the West we tend to associate this belief with cultures of the Far East, but in fact it has been found among the tribes of east and west Africa, the Inuit of the Arctic, the native tribes of northwest North America, the Aboriginal Australians, and many other widely separated cultures around the world.

At one time the belief in reincarnation was common in parts of the Western world, among the Pythagoreans of ancient Greece, the Celts of Great Britain, and the Vikings of Scandinavia. We have also seen earlier that at least some Christians believed in reincarnation, at least until the Council of Constantinople in 553 AD, which, as mentioned earlier, was called by the emperor, and which Pope Vigilius refused to attend, leading some to argue that it therefore should not be considered a valid council and an official ban.

How did reincarnation come to be such a widespread belief? The most plausible explanation comes from extensive reports of children who claim to recall a previous life. There are several ancient accounts of such claims from around the world, and between 1900 and 1960 a number of cases, mostly from India, were reported in books and other media. But most of the modern interest in this topic comes from the work of psychiatry professor Ian Stevenson, who in the 1950s began to collect and systematically compare such accounts. In 1960 he wrote a groundbreaking article, and in 1961 he received a grant to travel to India in order to more thoroughly investigate such cases.

Nothing prepared Stevenson for the abundance of cases he found there, and in 1966 he published his landmark book *Twenty Cases Suggestive of Reincarnation*. Since then, he has followed up with other books and numerous articles.

Stevenson used the standard investigative methods used by lawyers and historians. He would first interview the subject of the investigation and all firsthand witnesses. Usually, he held repeated interviews with the central informants in order to check the consistency of their reports and to study details previously missed. Not content to rely solely upon eyewitness testimony, Stevenson also located and copied birth certificates, hospital records, and reports of postmortem examinations in order to substantiate details of the eyewitness accounts.

The typical case involves a child between the ages of two and five who one day begins to speak of a previous life. The child will often use adult expressions and behave in a way that is strange for a child, but which seems entirely appropriate for the previous personality. The memories of the previous life usually begin to fade by ages five or six, and are usually gone by age eight, although there are exceptions to this rule.

One of the most prominent features of Stevenson's cases is the high incidence of violent death among the previous personalities. In 725 cases from six different cultures, Stevenson and his colleagues found that 61 percent of subjects remembered lives that ended violently.[108]

Another prominent feature of Stevenson's cases seems to be a sense of unfinished business in the lives of most of the previous personalities—even of the minority who died a natural death. Considering the majority of his cases, Stevenson writes:

> We can see that…their lives ended in a state of incompleteness. At the time of death they might all, for different reasons, have felt entitled to a longer life than the one they had had, and this in turn might have generated a craving for rebirth, perhaps leading to a quicker reincarnation than that among persons who died replete with life, so to speak, and at its natural end.[109]

Let us now consider one of the best-documented cases that Stevenson has collected.

The Case of Bishen Chand

Bishen Chand was born in 1921, in Bareilly, India. As he gradually gained the power of speech, he began to speak of a previous life in Pilibhit, a town approximately fifty kilometers to the east. He claimed his name had been Laxmi Narain, the son of a wealthy landowner, and even boasted how the influence of his family had enabled him to escape a charge of murder. He had a quick temper; his behavior was that of a spoiled young man, and he would frequently rebuke his parents for their poverty.

Through a friend the case came to the attention of K. Sahay, a prominent attorney in Bareilly, who visited the family in 1926 and wrote down twenty-one statements the boy made about his previous life. A few months later, not quite eight years after the death

---

108. Stevenson, *Children Who Remember Previous Lives,* 117, 160.
109. Stevenson, *Children Who Remember Previous Lives,* 212.

of Laxmi Narain, Sahay took Bishen and his father to Pilibhit, where he made additional statements about the life of Laxmi; only one of the twenty-one statements turned out to be wrong: the name of Har Narain was given correctly, but turned out to be Laxmi's father, not his uncle. He also recognized, without prompting, eight persons and places known to Laxmi Narain. The mother was still living; after asking the boy a series of test questions, she became convinced Bishen was her surviving son.

When the boy was presented with a set of *tabla* drums, he surprised his family by playing them skillfully, as Laxmi had been fond of doing. His father testified that Bishen had never even seen tabla before.

Bishen's older brother testified that when Bishen was a child, he could read Urdu, despite having had no instruction; his father, in a sworn statement, stated that Bishen as a child used some Urdu words. Laxmi Narain was well-educated and could speak Urdu.

This case was also independently investigated in detail by Stevenson, who considers the case of considerable evidential importance. Numerous statements had been written down by a prominent attorney before any verification was attempted. Many people who had personally known Laxmi Narain were still alive and were able to verify the accuracy of Bishen's claims. Two skills known to have been acquired by the previous personality were shown: playing the tabla drums and speaking Urdu, and there seems to have been no way that Bishen could have acquired these skills in any normal fashion.

As mentioned, as a child, Bishen behaved as a spoiled young man and would frequently boast of a murder he remembered committing. But as he grew older, his attitude gradually changed: it occurred to him that perhaps he had been reborn into poverty because of the murder that he had committed. He became a reformed person, and when Stevenson met him, Bishen showed remorse, and no signs of the violent behavior, debauchery, and haughtiness of Laxmi Narain. On the contrary, Stevenson considered him a kind and generous person of limited means.[110]

Fraud as an explanation can be ruled out: there was no possibility of anticipated financial gain, as it was well known that the Narain family had become destitute after Laxmi's death. And why would a father want his son to rebuke him for his poverty and boast of committing a murder?

There is only one remaining alternative explanation for the best cases that does not involve reincarnation: the child unconsciously employs extrasensory perception in order to unconsciously impersonate a deceased person they have never met.

But there are several problems:

- The children almost never show *any* evidence of ESP, apart from memories of a previous life.
- Information acquired telepathically or clairvoyantly is not typically experienced as something remembered—and certainly not as the memory of another person who lived before.
- In most real-life cases, the operation of ESP appears to be goal oriented. Yet there is no obvious motive in many cases of the children recalling a previous life; on the contrary, the strange behavior of the child often causes problems with his or her family.
- ESP cannot explain why subjects have difficulty recognizing persons or places that have changed since the death of the previous personality and cannot explain why the subjects

---

110. This case is described in detail in Stevenson, *Cases of the Reincarnation Type,* 176–205.

are unaware of changes in the previous personality's environment they have not yet seen.

- There is not merely information provided about the deceased; rather we have the *successful impersonation* of a deceased person the child has never met, and the *display of skills* the child has never acquired, yet were known to have been acquired by the deceased. Perception may enable someone to know *that* something is true, but not *how* to do something requiring intensive practice.

These problems should make obvious the strained and *ad hoc* nature of any explanation of the children's memories in terms of ESP.

We will now consider the most convincing single line of evidence for survival.

Chapter 9

Messages from the Dead

The idea that we can communicate with spirits is an ancient belief found among many societies past and present. In tribal cultures, one of the roles of the shaman, witchdoctor, or seer was to communicate with discarnate entities. Such individuals were often selected for their special role based upon their perceived ability to act as intermediaries between the spirit world and their tribe.

As Western culture has relentlessly encroached upon traditional societies, first-person accounts from tribal cultures are increasingly difficult to find. However, historical records show that there is a curiously consistent testimony to the genuineness of the phenomenon in the confessions of former shamans who had been converted to Christianity. Years later, they would not recant their former belief that the spirit phenomena had been genuine.

In 1863, William Howitt gave an example provided by a German missionary who had lived among the Native Americans. Years earlier, he had been baffled by the phenomena he had observed during a seance with a medicine man. Historian Brian Inglis writes:

Hearing thirty years later that the medicine man had become a Christian, the missionary thought that at last he would be able to find out how the trick had been done; but no. 'Believe me,' the medicine man told him, with evident sincerity, 'I did not deceive you; I did not shake the lodge; it was shaken by the power of the spirits.' Nor, he insisted, had he employed a 'double tongue'—ventriloquism. 'I only repeated what the spirits said to me. I heard their voices. The top of the lodge was full of them, and before me the sky and wide lands lay expanded; I could see great distances around me; and I believed I could recognize the most distant objects.'[111]

Similar accounts of mediumship and spirit possession have been gathered from traditional cultures around the world, including not only Native America but also Africa, China, and Nepal.[112] It is sometimes said that communication with the dead via mediums was rarely reported prior to the start of the modern Spiritualist movement in 1848, but this remark holds true primarily for Western Europe, where atypical constraints have operated. There seems to be every reason to believe that mediumistic communication with the dead has been practiced for centuries in non-European cultures. In his comprehensive 1933 work *Life Beyond Death in the Beliefs of Mankind*, Professor James Thayer Addison surveyed several ancient cultures and wrote:

In records of ancient Babylonia which cite the various orders of priests are listed "the inquirer of the dead" and "he who raises the spirits of the dead." In Gabun today the fetish doctor calls up the spirits by the sound of his little bell, interprets to them the requests of the living, and returns with the revelation of their consent or refusal. A similar type of medicine-man

---

111. Inlgis, *Natural and Supernatural*, 40.
112. See Gauld, *Mediumship and Survival*, 17.

now serves among the Maoris of New Zealand and the Pelew Islanders, for when he goes into a trance the ghosts can speak through him. Wang Ch'uang, the clever skeptic of first-century China, had been watching just such a ceremony when he wrote "Among men the dead speak through living persons whom they throw into a trance, and the wizards thrumming their black chords, call down souls of the dead, who can then speak through the mouths of the wizards."[113]

Although accounts of mediumship come from ancient, traditional, and non-Western cultures throughout the world, it was not until the late nineteenth century that this phenomenon began to be rigorously studied by some of the most prominent intellectuals of the Western world. These efforts began with the founding of the British Society for Psychical Research by philosopher Henry Sidgwick at Cambridge in 1882, and with the founding of the American Society for Psychical Research by philosopher William James at Harvard in 1884.

These investigations began with a study of both mental mediumship and physical mediumship, the latter involving the seeming production of various physical phenomena. But after members of the Society for Psychic Research (SPR) exposed several fraudulent physical mediums, the study of physical mediumship was abandoned, as the reports could easily be dismissed on grounds of fraud or mistaken eyewitness testimony.

The investigators then concentrated on mental mediumship, in which the medium goes into a trance, and then either writes messages or conveys them verbally. The rarest and most dramatic form of mental mediumship is possession mediumship, in which a departed mind appears to take full possession of the medium's

---

113. Quoted in Hart, *The Enigma of Survival*, 256–7.

vocal cords and body. As a matter of policy, the SPR routinely kept complete records of everything written and said during seances, and so questions of mistaken eyewitness testimony, faulty memory, and exaggeration simply do not arise.

The other lines of evidence so far considered depend, more or less, on eyewitness accounts, and so there is always the possibility of malobservation, exaggeration, faulty memory, and so on. With the evidence from mediumship as gathered by the careful investigators of the SPR on both sides of the Atlantic, these possibilities simply do not exist. Everything said and written during the seances was recorded, and so we have the permanent and objective evidence of the documents.

Initial findings on mediumship were promising, although counterexplanations were soon raised. The SPR investigated the best mediums in minute detail, and even hired detectives to secretly trail several of them, with the result that even the slightest suspicion of fraud was soon ruled out. It also soon became clear that from cases in which the medium did not know the sitter, the amount of highly accurate information vastly exceeded what could be expected by chance.[114]

Another explanation proposed was that the medium "fishes" for information, using a combination of guesswork and hints from the reactions of sitters. A less conventional explanation was that the results were due to an unusual degree of telepathic rapport between medium and sitter.

Proxy sittings—in which a sitter with no connection to the deceased visits the medium on behalf of a third person—were used to eliminate both these possibilities. The best known of these proxy sittings are the numerous ones in which the Reverend

---

114. See Carter, *Science and the Afterlife*, chapter 12.

Drayton Thomas acted as proxy, usually on behalf of bereaved parents and spouses. One such sitting was arranged by Professor E. R. Dodds, a well-known critic of the evidence for survival. The sitting was not on behalf of Dodds, but rather for a Mrs. Lewis who wished to contact her deceased father, and so the sitting was not even secondhand, but thirdhand. Thomas was told only the man's name, hometown, and date of death. Regardless, at a sitting the medium seemed to get in touch with him right away, and the results were considered very impressive.[115] Dodds, the skeptical investigator, was forced to conclude:

> It appears to me that the hypothesis of fraud, rational influence from disclosed facts, telepathy from the actual sitter, and coincidence cannot either singly or in combination account for the results obtained. Only the barest information was supplied to sitter and medium, and that through an indirect channel.[116]

Not only is there no experimental evidence for such an indirect form of telepathy, but both experimental and anecdotal evidence strongly suggest that telepathy usually operates between people who are emotionally linked, or at least associated in some way.

For example, from his experiments with telephone telepathy, Sheldrake concluded:

> In some of our tests, there were two familiar callers and two unfamiliar callers whom the subjects had never met but whose names they knew. The hit rate with unfamiliar callers was near the chance level; with the familiar callers it was 52 per cent, about twice the chance level. This experiment supported the

115. Carter, *Science and the Afterlife*, 166.
116. Carter, *Science and the Afterlife*, 167.

idea that telepathy occurs more between people who are bonded to each other than between strangers.[117]

The same conclusion has been drawn from the Ganzfeld telepathy experiments (in which the chance success rate is 25 percent). In one large-scale study the average hit rate was 37 percent when the senders and receivers were emotionally close, versus 27 percent for the general population.[118] And, the investigators found that "parent/child and sibling sender-receiver pairs produced exceptionally high hit rates, 43.5% and 71.4% respectively."[119]

But what emotional link was there between the proxy sitter and medium with relatives and friends of the deceased? In a word, *none*. Yet a volume of ESP far exceeding in accuracy and detail that found in any experiment ever attempted is alleged to have occurred between people with no connection whatsoever.

Noting the contrived nature of telepathic explanations of mediumship, Thomas wrote:

> Critics who wish to apply the telepathic hypothesis will need to assume, without any justification for such an assumption, that thoughts pass between people who have not heard of each other and between whom there is no link save that they were interested in a person who died. And further, the selection must be assumed to act with unerring discretion, so that no facts are allowed to pass which do not relate to the inquiry at hand. In short, *everything must happen exactly as if* an intelligent supervisor were obtaining information from the deceased for the purposes of the inquiry.[120]

---

117. Sheldrake, *The Science Delusion*, 245.
118. Broughton and Alexander, "Autoganzfeld II," 118.
119. Broughton and Alexander, "Autoganzfeld II," 218.
120. Thomas, "A Proxy Extending over Eleven Sittings with Mrs. Osborne Leonard," 502–3.

The difficulties of using extrasensory perception (ESP) as an explanation of the best cases resulted in the hypothesis of *Super-ESP*—that is, ESP (telepathy and clairvoyance) of a range, power, and accuracy far exceeding that found in experimental or anecdotal reports.

Telepathy and clairvoyance involve the transfer of information, but the minds of living persons involve much more than mere memories of their lives; they also have purposes, perspective, personalities, and skills.

Purpose Contrary to That of Medium or Sitter

Several cases on record clearly show evidence of the purpose of the deceased communicator. One such case comes from prerevolutionary Russia, reported by Alexander Aksakov, imperial councilor to the czar.

In January 1885, Aksakov's sister-in-law Mrs. A. von Wiesler and her daughter Sophie began to experiment with a pointer and an alphabet written on paper, when they suddenly received a message from "Schura," who claimed to be the deceased daughter of distant acquaintances, and who had held revolutionary views. Schura had ended her life with poison at the age of seventeen a few weeks earlier, after the arrest and execution of a like-minded and much-loved male cousin. She now warned that another cousin of hers, Nikolaus, had also fallen in with a band of radicals, and that his family needed to be warned of the great danger. However, Sophie and her mother expressed hesitation for reasons of social propriety. "Absurd ideas of propriety!" was "Schura's" indignant reply.

All of this was very characteristic of the living Schura, who had been very decisive, forceful, and who had come to despise the conventions of society. However, Sophie and her mother continued to hesitate, while "Schura's" demands for them to act became more and more vehement, until finally, on February 26, she wrote, "It is too late … expect his arrest."

Nikolaus was later arrested and exiled because of political assemblies he had attended in January and February 1885—the very months in which "Schura" had been insisting that steps should be taken *immediately* to dissuade Nikolaus from taking part in such meetings.

The operation of extrasensory perception in real-life almost always seems goal directed, operating in order to fulfill some purpose or interest of the person having the perception. Yet in this case the purpose of the communications received was definitely not that of the operators of the planchette board (who functioned as both mediums *and* sitters). This is an example of a "drop-in" communicator, and one who was known only slightly to the von Wieslers. And, since they knew the other family only slightly, the thought of contacting them about so intimate a family matter embarrassed them. However, the purpose shown in the communications would certainly have been that of the living Schura, if she had known of the danger to Nikolaus.

Perspective of the Deceased

One of the most impressive trance mediums investigated by the SPR on both sides of the Atlantic was Leonora Piper of Boston. Richard Hodgson, lawyer, philosopher, and skeptical member of the SPR, had debunked several fraudulent mediums and was determined to debunk Piper. He had her trailed by detectives and even brought her to England where she knew no one, and so could have no confederates. The successes continued. Impressed,

Hodgson joined the SPR as a full-time researcher, and spent the last eighteen years of his life studying Miss Piper.

In 1893 Hodgson arranged two sittings with Reverend S. W. Sutton and his wife, in which their deceased daughter Katherine (who called herself "Kakie") communicated. Piper spoke through a "control," that is, a seemingly discarnate person who acted as an intermediary. In this case the control was the usual Dr. Phinuit, who claimed to be a deceased French physician.

"Kakie" communicated naturally and accurately with the sitters, at one point hushing singers to finish four lines of a song alone:

[I asked if she remembered anything after she was brought downstairs.] I was so hot, my head was so hot. [Correct.]…[I asked if she suffered in dying.] I saw the light and followed it to this pretty lady…Do not cry for me—that makes me sad. Eleanor. I want Eleanor. [Her little sister. She called her much during her last illness.] I want my buttons. Row, row—my song—sing it now. I sing with you. [We sing, and a soft child voice sings with us.]

> Lightly row, lightly row,
> O'er the merry waves we go,
> Smoothly glide, smoothly glide,
> With the ebbing tide.

[Phinuit hushes us, and Kakie finishes alone.]

> Let the wind and waters be
> Mingled with our melody,
> Sing and float, sing and float
> In our little boat.[121]

---

121. Hodgson, "A Further Record," 485–6.

In his review of this case, researcher Dr. Alan Gauld concluded, "I know of no instance of undeniable telepathy between living persons, or for that matter of any variety of ESP, in which the flow of paranormally acquired information has been so quick, so copious, and so free from error."[122] Yet none of the information conveyed was unknown to the sitters. However, one of the difficulties in using ESP to explain this case is that during both sittings several associations were made that were not in the minds of the adults, but rather in the mind of the child. For instance, the Kakie communicator asked at one point for a toy horse. From the transcript of the sitting:

> Kakie wants the horse. [I gave him the little horse she played with during her illness.] No, that is not the one. The big horse—so big [Phinuit shows how large]. Eleanor's horse. Eleanor used to put it in Kakie's lap. [This horse was packed, in Trenton, and had not occurred to me in connection with Kakie. What she said of it was true.][123]

Gauld commented on what these passages imply:

> If we are to say that Mrs. Piper could select from the sitters' minds associations conflicting with the ones consciously present and utilize them in order to create the impression that the communicator's thoughts moved along lines distinctively different from the sitter's, we are beginning to attribute to her not just super-ESP but super-artistry as well.[124]

Another trance medium studied by the SPR was Mrs. Gladys Leonard, whom the SPR also had shadowed by detectives. Not a trace of fraud was ever found. Leonard's usual control was named Feda, who claimed to be the spirit of a deceased Native American

122. Gauld, *Mediumship and Survival*, 41.
123. Hodgson, "A Further Record," 491. Also see Carter, *Science and the Afterlife*, 181–2.
124. Gauld, *Mediumship and Survival*, 42.

girl. An odd feature of Leonard's mediumship is that when Feda was in control and relaying messages from another communicator, she would sometimes be interrupted by a whisper seeming to come from the empty air directly in front of the medium. This "direct voice" seemed to be that of the communicator, and would sometimes interrupt and correct mistakes in Feda's statements. At times the direct voice appears to express frustration with Feda, as though irritated by the effort of trying to dictate to a rather obtuse secretary.

> FEDA: He says that the pheno*meter*—phenomena—He's got a thermometer!
>
> D. V.: *I was not talking about thermometers!*
>
> FEDA: Oh, he says, phenomena. Is that right? The phenomena referred to.[125]
>
> FEDA: Your father says—
>
> D. V.: *A few days out!*
>
> FEDA: A few days out? What, out of bed?
>
> D. V.: *No, no, no no!*
>
> FEDA: A few days out? Oh, I'll tell him. He was a few days out in his reckoning about the war.[126]

On another occasion:

> FEDA: He says you must have good working—What? Hippopotamuses?
>
> D. V.: *Hypotheses.*
>
> FEDA: (more loudly) Hippopotamuses.
>
> D. V.: *Hypotheses—and don't shout!*
>
> FEDA: I'm not shouting. I'm only speaking plainly.[127]

---

125. Thomas, "A New Hypothesis Concerning Trance Communications," 143.
126. Thomas, "A New Hypothesis," 142.
127. Thomas, "A New Hypothesis," 143.

These examples create an obvious difficulty for the hypothesis of telepathy from the living, for there is no evidence that telepathically received information is ever first received wrongly, and then *corrected*. But mistakes and subsequent corrections make perfect sense if the messages are in fact what they purport to be.

So far, we have seen examples of communications that not only involve *information* far exceeding in speed and accuracy what's found in laboratory and anecdotal reports of extrasensory perception: we have also seen examples that require clever and cunning *deception* by the medium's unconscious mind, in order to present the information with the *purpose* and from the *perspective* of only the deceased. And even this *ad hoc* addition of elaborate and unconscious deception is not enough to explain the next set of cases.

Personality *and* Perspective

We have already seen several examples in which the distinctive personality of the deceased appears evident in the communications. The following remarks, fairly typical, were made after sittings with Mrs. Piper in which deceased friends of the sitters gave every appearance of speaking directly through the medium:

> The clearly-marked personality of the friend, whom I will call T., is to me the most convincing proof of Mrs. P.'s supernatural power, but it is a proof impossible to present to anyone else.

Another sitter remarked:

> In a great many little ways he is quite like what my friend used to be when living, so much so that I am afraid it would take a great deal of explanation to make me believe that his identical self had not something to do with it, wholly apart from

the medium's powers or from anything that may be in my own mind concerning him.[128]

After the death of Dr. A. W. Verrall, messages purporting to come from him were received through the English medium Mrs. Willet, and Verrall's close friend Reverend M. A. Bayfield commented on the messages:

All this is Verrall's manner to the life in animated conversation … When I first read the words quoted above I received a series of little shocks, for the turns of speech are Verrall's, the high-pitched emphasis is his, and I could hear the very tones in which he would have spoken each sentence.[129]

An intimate friend of Verrall's agreed with Bayfield's assessment, as did his surviving wife and a niece of Verrall's. Bayfield continued:

We have here an extraordinary faithful representation of Verrall in respect of a peculiar kind of impatience and a habit of emphasis which he had in conversation, and of his playfulness and sense of humour … to me at least it is incredible that even the cleverest could achieve such an unexampled triumph in deceptive impersonation as this would be if the actor is not Verrall himself.[130]

Mrs. Willett ("Mrs. Willett" was a pseudonym for Mrs. Coombe-Tennant, justice of the peace and the first woman to be appointed by the British Government as a delegate to the assembly of the League of Nations) did meet the living Verrall three times, although the acquaintance seems to have been slight, as none of the

---

128. Hodgson, "A Further Record," 290.
129. Bayfield, "Notes on the Same Scripts," 246.
130. Bayfield, "Notes on the Same Scripts," 249.

investigators thought that she knew him intimately at all. However, in the next case involving Mrs. Piper and George Pellew, the relationship was even slighter, as Piper had met the living Pellew only once, when he attended a seance under an assumed name.

We mentioned earlier that Hodgson began his investigations as a die-hard skeptic and debunker of fraudulent mediums, only to change his mind after investigating Mrs. Piper. The turning point came after the accidental death of his close friend George Pellew at age thirty-two. Pellew, who was extremely skeptical about survival, did however promise Hodgson that if he died first and found himself still living, he would try to communicate.

About four weeks after his death, Hodgson attended a sitting with Piper along with another close friend of Pellew who visited under an assumed name. With Phinuit acting as intermediary, messages purporting to come from George Pellew (these messages will here be attributed to "GP") were given along with his full name and the correct name of the close friend present. Incidents unknown to Hodgson and the friend were discussed, which concerned another family, the Howards. Three weeks later another seance was held with Mr. Howard and his wife, and after Phinuit said a few words, GP suddenly appeared to control Piper's voice directly. Many private matters were discussed, and Hodgson wrote that the Howards "were profoundly impressed with the feeling that they were in truth holding a conversation with the personality of the friend whom they had known so many years."[131]

From this time on, GP communicated directly through Mrs. Piper's voice, or by writing with her hand.

As a test, 150 different sitters were introduced to GP, of whom the living George Pellew knew only 30. GP correctly recognized

---

131. Hodgson, "A Further Record," 300.

by name 29 of the 30 that George Pellew had known in life (the sole exception was a young woman whom we will soon meet). Conversations were in a manner appropriate for the living Pellew's relationship with the individual sitter, and GP always showed an intimate knowledge of Pellew's past relationships with them. As Hodgson wrote, in each case "the recognition was clear and full, and accompanied by an appreciation of the relations which subsisted between GP living and the sitters."[132] And there was not a single case of false recognition: that is, GP never once greeted anyone of the 120 that the living Pellew had *not* known.

Hodgson added:

> The continual manifestation of this personality—so different from Phinuit or other communicators—with its own reservoir of memories, with its swift appreciation of any reference to friends of GP, with its "give and take" in little incidental conversations with myself, has helped largely in producing a conviction of the actual presence of the GP personality, which it would be quite impossible to impart by any mere enumeration of verifiable statements.[133]

It was the continual manifestation of this personality that finally drove Hodgson to conclude beyond reasonable doubt that Piper was genuine. Hodgson was convinced that Piper had no knowledge of the living Pellew; yet how could she have succeeded in dramatically impersonating someone she had barely met over four years earlier in a manner that convinced thirty people that they were indeed conversing with their old friend?[134]

---

132. Hodgson, "A Further Record," 328.
133. Hodgson, "A Further Record," 328.
134. Hodgson was not the only investigator who studied Mrs. Piper with the intent of debunking her. Dr. James Hyslop, quoted at the opening of this book, also changed his mind after studying Mrs. Piper.

Hodgson finally admitted:

> I had but one object, to discover fraud and trickery. Frankly, I went to Mrs. Piper with Professor James of Harvard University about twelve years ago with the object of unmasking her. I entered the house profoundly materialistic, not believing in the continuance of life after death; today I say I believe. The truth has been given to me in such a way as to remove from me the possibility of doubt.[135]

We can see in these cases that we are beginning to require something different *in kind* from extrasensory perception. Even if we grant—for the sake of argument—that the medium possesses the staggeringly vast powers of ESP required to *instantly* telepathically or clairvoyantly acquire the facts needed in these conversations, there is still a vast difference between *knowing mere facts* about a person, and then translating those facts into a completely lifelike impersonation of someone unknown or barely known to the actor. An entirely different skill is required, and this skill cannot be reduced to a mere knowledge of facts, however those facts may have been acquired.

Allan Gauld illustrates the difference with an example from his own research:

> Some 10 or 12 years ago I spent a good deal of time studying the papers and diaries or FWH Myers and Henry Sidgwick, thus learning a good many intimate details about their lives, characters, friends, families, and domestic arrangements. Yet I could no more deploy this accumulated knowledge to develop impersonations of them which would have passed muster before their close friends than I could fly. The gap between

---

135. Quoted in Tweedale, *Man's Survival After Death*, 470.

accumulating such knowledge and deploying it in the construction of a realistic communicator is enormous.[136]

It therefore seems that not even highly detailed knowledge, gathered by *any* form of perception, extrasensory or otherwise, is enough to account for the completely lifelike impersonation of Pellew over a period of five years.

And there is a final point to be made with regard to the Pellew communications. Recall from above that GP failed to recognize only one of the thirty sitters who had known the living Pellew, a young woman who had been a child when the living Pellew knew her mother.

At the first sitting Miss Warner held with Mrs. Piper, Phinuit was the predominant control, and GP communicated briefly at the end of the sitting to ask about an old friend of his named Rogers.

The next day, Miss Warner attended a second sitting with Hodgson also in attendance, and GP asked who she was. The following exchange then occurred:

I do not think I knew you very well. (Very little. You used to come and see my mother.) I heard of you, I suppose. (I saw you several times. You used to come with Mr. Rogers.) Yes, I remembered about Mr. Rogers when I saw you before. (Yes, you spoke of him.) Yes, but I cannot seem to place you. I long to place all of my friends, and could do so before I had been gone so long. You see I am farther away … I do not recall your face. You must have changed … (R. H.: Do you remember Mrs. Warner?) Of course, oh, very well. For pity sake are you her little daughter? (Yes.) By Jove, how you have grown … I thought so much of your mother, a charming woman. (She always enjoyed seeing you, I know.) I wish I could have known you

---

136. Gauld, "Discarnate Survival," 620–1.

better, it would have been so nice to have recalled the past. (I was a little girl.)[137]

Since Miss Warner had changed a great deal in the eight years since the living Pellew had last seen her, the nonrecognition by George Pellew would have been perfectly natural.

However, on the hypothesis of telepathy, there is no explanation for GP's failure to recognize Miss Warner. Since both Miss Warner and Hodgson were aware that the living Pellew knew her when she was a child, sources for telepathy were readily at hand, and here the ESP hypothesis would predict "recognition." On the other hand, the *non*recognition of Miss Warner is precisely what would be expected if Pellew were in fact directly communicating.

---

137. Hodgson, "A Further Record," 324–5.

Chapter 10
Display of Skills

Next, we will consider cases in which the medium clearly displayed high-level skills she did not possess, yet were most certainly possessed by the deceased. These cases are even more difficult to explain than displays of the purpose, perspective, and personality of the deceased.

The first example comes from the mediumship of the English medium Mrs. Willet. When she went into a trance, she did not appear to lose control of her body; rather, she would sit up and talk in a natural way. Messages appeared to be conveyed directly to her, which she would then pass on to sitters.

Her two main communicators appeared to be Edmund Gurney and Frederic Myers, both of whom in life were avid philosophers and founders of the SPR. Through Mrs. Willet the alleged communicators Gurney and Myers requested sittings with their friend GW Balfour, who had engaged in numerous philosophical discussions with Gurney and Myers before they died.

With Willet in a trance, lively philosophical discussions would ensue, and the communicators showed a thorough acquaintance with the views and terminology of books written by the living Myers and Gurney. This was in the format of conversational give-and-take, not merely the outpouring of views. The philosopher CD Broad wrote that the communications were "plainly the product of a highly intelligent mind or minds, with a keen interest in psychology, psychical research and philosophy, and with a capacity for drawing subtle and significant distinctions."[138] The philosopher Robert Almeder wrote that some of the sittings "were purely philosophical and sound like the transcript of an Ivy League graduate seminar on classical philosophy."[139]

The ESP hypothesis is strained by Mrs. Willet's mediumship in two crucial ways:

First, although Mrs. Willet had never met the living Myers or Gurney, several of their close friends and acquaintances were convinced that the Myers and Gurney communicators acted and spoke in ways uniquely characteristic of Myers and Gurney. Balfour found the communications so convincing and natural that he came to believe he was indeed communicating with his old friends Myers and Gurney.

Second—and perhaps even more startling—Mrs. Willet was neither educated nor interested in philosophy, and showed little patience for such discussions. Boredom and bewilderment best describe the attitude of her own personality toward the communications, both in trance and out. At one point she complained, "You see it seems a long time since I was here with them and I want to talk and enjoy myself. And I've all the time, to keep on working, and seeing and listening to such boring old—Oh Ugh!" At another point, the Gurney personality was discussing in detail some phil-

138. Broad, *Lectures on Psychical Research*, 297.
139. Almeder, *Death & Personal Survival*, 219.

osophical problem, and she exclaimed "Oh, Edmund, you do *bore* me so!"[140]

The next case involves the high-level display of another skill.

In 1855 Judge John Worth Edmonds, president of the New York State Senate and later Justice of the Supreme Court of New York, reported a case involving a trance medium who spoke in a language in which she was entirely ignorant, and in this language conveyed correct information unknown to anyone present.

The judge began his investigations into mediumship as a determined debunker; so, imagine his surprise when his daughter Laura began to shine as a developing medium. One of her most impressive gifts was an ability to "speak in many tongues," as he put it.

> She knows no language but her own, and a little smattering of boarding-school French; yet she has spoken in nine or ten different tongues, sometimes for an hour at a time, with the ease and fluency of a native. It is not unfrequent that foreigners converse with their Spirit friends, through her, in their own language. A recent instance occurred, where a Greek gentleman had several interviews, and for several hours at a time carried on the conversation on his part in Greek, and received his answers sometimes in that language, and sometimes in English. Yet, until then, she had never heard a word of modern Greek spoken.[141]

A few years later Edmonds elaborated on the seance with the Greek gentleman.

> The incident with the Greek gentleman as this: One evening, when some twelve or fifteen people were in my parlor, Mr. E. D. Green, an artist of the city, was shown in, accompanied by a

---

140. Heywood, *Beyond the Reach of Sense*, 102.
141. Edmonds, *Spiritualism*, 45.

gentleman whom he introduced as Mr. Evangelides. He spoke broken English, and Greek fluently. Ere long, a Spirit spoke to him through Laura, in English, and said so many things to him, that he identified him as a friend who had died at his house a few years before, but of whom none of us had ever heard.

Occasionally, through Laura, the Spirit would speak a word or a sentence in Greek, until Mr. E inquired if he could be understood if he spoke in Greek? The residue of the conversation, for more than an hour, was, on his part entirely in Greek, and on hers, sometimes in Greek and sometimes in English.

He was sometimes very much affected, so much so as to attract the attention of the company, some of whom begged to know what it was that caused so much emotion. He declined to tell, but after the conversation ended, he told us that he had never before witnessed any Spirit manifestations, and that he had, during the conversation, tried experiments to test that which was so novel to him. These experiments were in speaking of subjects which he knew Laura must be ignorant of, and in frequently and suddenly changing the topic from domestic to political affairs, from philosophy to theology, and so on. In answer to our inquiries—for none of us knew Greek—he assured us that his Greek must have been understood, and her Greek was correct.[142]

Years after this, Edmonds explained why Evangelides had been so emotionally affected by what Laura had said.

One evening I had a visit from a stranger, a Greek named Evangelides; it was not long before he was speaking to Laura in his own tongue. In the course of the conversation he seemed greatly affected, and even shed tears. Six or seven people were present, and one of them asked the reason for his emotion.

---

142. Edmonds, *Letters and Tracts on Spiritualism*, 70–71.

The Greek avoided a direct reply, saying that it was a question of family matters.

On the next day he renewed his conversation with Laura, and since there were no strangers in my house this time, he gave us the desired explanation. The invisible personality with whom he was speaking, with Laura as an intermediary, said that he was an intimate friend, who had died in Greece, the brother of the Greek patriot, Marco Bozarris. The friend informed Evangelides of the death of his (Evangelides') son, who had stayed in Greece and had been in excellent health when his father left for America.

Ten days after his first visit Evangelides informed us that he had just received a letter telling him of the death of his son. The letter must have been on its way at the time of his first interview with Laura.[143]

Judge Edmonds made the following observations about what happened during the seance:

To deny the fact is impossible, it was too well known; I could as well deny the light of the sun; nor could I think it an illusion, for it is in no way different from any other reality. It took place before ten educated and intelligent persons. We had never seen Mr. Evangelides before; he was introduced by a friend that same evening. How could Laura tell him of his son? How could she understand and speak Greek which she had never previously heard?[144]

The next case also involves the demonstration of a skill, and this at a level very few people in the world possess.

---

143. Lomaxe, "Judge Edmonds: A Psychic Sensitive," 11–12.
144. Quoted in Almeder, *Death & Personal Survival*, 206.

Chess Game with
a Deceased Grand Master

The remarkable story of a chess game played between a living and a deceased grand master began in 1985, when chess enthusiast Dr. Wolfgang Eisenbeiss decided to initiate a chess match between living and deceased grand masters. He contacted Romanian-born musician, composer, and amateur medium Robert Rollans, who always offered his services as a medium free of charge. Eisenbeiss had known Rollans for eight years, and trusted his assertion that he did not know how to play chess.

Eisenbeiss was able to persuade the world-famous chess champion Victor Korchnoi, then ranked third in the world, to participate. Korchnoi was described in *Chessbase* (April 4, 2002) as "unquestionably one of the great chess players of all time."

Eisenbeiss then gave Rollans a list of deceased grand masters and asked him to find one willing to play. On June 15, 1985, a communicator claiming to be deceased Hungarian grand master Geza Maroczy agreed to play. Maroczy was ranked third in the world in 1900 and was known for his remarkably strong endgame.

The Maroczy communicator provided his motivation for participating in the game as follows:

> I will be at your disposal in this peculiar game of chess for two reasons. First, because I also want to do something to aid mankind living on earth to become convinced that death does not end everything, but instead the mind is separated from the physical body and comes up to us in a new world, where individual life continues to manifest itself in a new unknown dimension. Second, being a Hungarian patriot I want to guide the eyes of the world into the direction of my beloved Hun-

gary a little bit. Both these items have convinced me to participate in that game with the thought of being at everyone's service.[145]

For the sake of simplicity, I will refer to "the communicator identifying himself as Maroczy" as simply Maroczy.

The entire game was played with Rollans in Germany, and with Eisenbeiss acting as intermediary, relaying the moves back and forth between Korchnoi and Rollans. At no time did Korchnoi and Rollans have direct contact, except for a handshake on a TV show in September 1992, four and a half months before the end of the game.

At the twenty-seventh move, Korchnoi commented on the quality of his opponent's play:

During the opening phase Maroczy showed weakness. His play is old-fashioned. But I must confess that my last moves have not been too convincing. I am not sure I will win. He has compensated the faults of the opening by a strong end-game. In the end-game the ability of a player shows up and my opponent plays very well.[146]

The game continued, always with Eisenbeiss as an intermediary, until 1993, when Maroczy resigned at move forty-eight. The long duration was due to Korchnoi's frequent travels (in the days before widespread email) and to Rollans's illness (Rollans died just nineteen days after Maroczy resigned).

The full match went as follows:

---

145. Eisenbeiss and Hassler, "An Assessment of Ostensible Communications with a Deceased Grandmaster as Evidence for Survival," 70.

146. Eisenbeiss and Hassler, "An Assessment of Ostensible Communications with a Deceased Grandmaster as Evidence for Survival," 67.

1. e4 e6	19. Qe4 Qxe4+	37. Rf5+ Kxg4
2. d4 d5	20. fxe4 f6	38. h6 b3
3. Nc3 Bb4	21. Rad1 e5	39. h7 Ra8
4. e5 c5	22. Rd3 Kf7	40. cxb3 Rh8
5. a3 Bxc3+	23. Rg3 Rg6	42. Rg6+ Kf4
6. bxc3 Ne7	24. Rhg1 Rag8	43. Rf6+ Kg3
7. Qg4 cxd4	25. a4 Rxg3	44. Rf1 Rh2
8. Qxg7 Rg8	26. fxg3 b6	45. Rd1 Kf3
9. Qxh7 Qc7	27. h4 a6	46. Rf1+ Rf2
10. Kd1 dxc3	28. g4 b5	47. Rfx2+ Kxf2
11. Nf3 Nbc6	29. axb5 axb5	0-1
12. Bb5 Bd7	30. Kd3 Kg6	Maroczy resigns
13. Bxc6 Bxc6	31. Rf1 Rh8	
14. Bg5 d4	32. Rh1 Rh7	
15. Bxe7 Kxe7	33. Ke2 Ra7	48. b4 c2
16. Qh4+ Ke8	34. Kd3 Ra2	49. Kxc2 Ke2
17. Ke2 Bxf3+	35. Rf1 b4	50. b5 d3+
18. gxf3 Qxe5+	36. h5+ Kg5	51. Kc3 d2
		52. b6 d1=Q[147]

Psychiatrist and former South African chess champion Vernon Neppe reanalyzed this case in 2007, with the aid of a chess-playing computer program. He wanted to answer these three questions:

---

147. Moves 48–52 show how the game would have played out and provide the reason Maroczy resigned at move 47.

1. At what level did Maroczy play this chess game?
2. Could a chess computer reproduce this game?
3. Was the Maroczy style something a computer could replicate?

Regarding level of play, Neppe concluded that "Maroczy played at least at the Master level, and debatably, at a rusty, lowish grandmaster level."[148] Neppe's only criticism of Maroczy's play was his weak opening, which both he and Korchnoi found old-fashioned. Other than that, "Maroczy, in my opinion, plays perfect chess."

We should also note the opinion of Bobby Fischer, considered one of the greatest chess players of all time. His brother-in-law, the physicist Russell Targ, examined this case, and wrote:

> I sent the reported final chess score to Bobby Fischer—who, as I mentioned earlier, lived in Iceland, having been rescued from a Japanese jail by the kindness of the Icelandic government. Bobby wrote to me, saying that, "anyone who can go fifty-two moves with Victor Korchnoi is playing at a grandmaster level."[149]

Neppe then tried to answer the question as to whether a computer could have simulated Maroczy's game. He set the program Sigma Chess 6.0 to respond to Korchnoi's moves and compared the computer's choices with those of *Maroczy*.

> Maroczy played human-type moves, and the computer simulation played computer-type moves correcting what it thought were inferior moves (e.g. in moves 23 and 24) despite their illogicality. Maroczy clearly played the endgame far better than the computer.[150]

148. Neppe, "A Detailed Analysis of an Important Chess Game," 146.
149. Targ, *Do You See What I See?*, 224.
150. Neppe, "A Detailed Analysis of an Important Chess Game," 136.

Neppe noted that the old-fashioned opening style of Maroczy's game also makes it unlikely that a computer was used to hoax the game. "This fact is important because it suggests that anyone hoaxing the game is unlikely to have done so with a computer."[151]

Comparing the style of Maroczy's game with the style of the computer's game, Neppe wrote:

> Maroczy played in a style reminiscent of the early twentieth century, and demonstrated the endgame expertise he was famous for…In any event, the differences in style between an accomplished chess player (like a grandmaster) and even the most remarkable computer hardware and software are profound.[152]

And we should note that this is not simply Neppe's personal opinion: philosopher and chess enthusiast Tim McGrew of Michigan University extensively analyzed the ability of computers using late-twentieth-century software to play chess, and has written, "Barring a conceptual breakthrough, computer chess is and will remain detectably inhuman."[153]

Considering the possibility of fraud with the use of a computer, Neppe concluded: "It is my opinion that a chess computer could not reproduce this game as of the 1980s. Nor is it likely that it could replicate Maroczy's play even today because of the stylistic elements."[154]

In other words, during the period of the game, computer technology—both software and hardware—were simply not advanced enough to give a chess grand master a challenging game. Also, it

---

151. Neppe, "A Detailed Analysis of an Important Chess Game," 142.
152. Neppe, "A Detailed Analysis of an Important Chess Game," 143.
153. McGrew, "The Simulation of Expertise: Deeper Blue and the Riddle of Cognition," 1998.
154. Neppe, "A Detailed Analysis of an Important Chess Game," 146.

is exceedingly unlikely that the software would be programed to use an old-fashioned opening. Finally, software cannot, even today, simulate a human style of play, and certainly cannot simulate the unique style of an accomplished player such as Geza Maroczy.

But there is even more to the case than demonstrated high-level chess skills. Maroczy, through Rollans, was asked eighty-one questions about the obscure life of Geza Maroczy; he answered seventy-nine (97.5 percent) correctly (two remained unsolved). And it is worth noting that many of Maroczy's answers to these questions were so difficult to authenticate that neither Eisenbeiss, Hassler, nor Korchnoi could answer them. In the end, Eisenbeiss employed a professional historian from Hungary—the historian-chess-player László Sebestyén—to track down the answers.[155] This historian consulted several libraries—the library of the Budapest Chess Club, Library of the Hungarian Parliament, Library of the Hungarian Scientific Academy—and questioned Maróczy's surviving two children.

It is further worth noting that the accuracy rate for the most difficult-to-answer questions was thirty-one out of thirty-one, 100 percent accuracy.

And as mentioned earlier, Eisenbeiss had known Rollans for eight years, and trusted him. Eisenbeiss and Hassler testified on behalf of Rollans's honesty:

> To the best of our knowledge, Mr. Rollans did not seek help (from persons or databases) concerning moves of the match or matters of chess history during the years of the match. Witnesses who attest to these circumstances and their continuation from the beginning to the end of the match are Dr. Eisenbeiss, Mrs. Ellen Rollans, Prof. Schiebeler and Mr. Holbe.

---

155. The historian was told it was for a Maroczy biography.

Mr. Rollans undertook his part of this endeavor on a voluntary, unpaid basis. His purpose in facilitating this match was his wish to prove that physical death is by no means the end of personal life.[156]

And yet, desperate to discredit this case, some materialists have raised the possibility that Rollans—a musician with an impeccable reputation for honesty, who never accepted payment for his services as a medium—spent his time between moves studying chess, secretly consulting with a chess master, and travelled from his home in Germany to conduct research in Hungarian libraries, all to pull off an elaborate hoax. For instance, archmaterialist Edwin May has written that there was "ample opportunity for Rollans to read up/consult on Maróczy's style/background."[157]

May provides not a single shred of evidence that Rollans committed fraud; he is content to simply raise the *logical possibility* of fraud, and leave it at that.

We have to take the word of Eisenbeiss that Rollans is not consulting someone else, thus violating the long-standing rules of parapsychological investigations—do not trust the participant at any time.[158]

So, what would satisfy May that fraud can be completely ruled out?

It would require at least one of the witnesses to be by the side of Rollans for 7.8 years to ensure that he did not seek outside assistance for this, or did not read anything about chess during

156. Eisenbeiss and Hassler, "An Assessment of Ostensible Communications with a Deceased Grandmaster as Evidence for Survival," 71.
157. May, "An alternative hypothesis for the Géza Maróczy (via medium Rollans) vs. Viktor Korchnoi chess game," 1.
158. May, "An alternative hypothesis for the Géza Maróczy (via medium Rollans) vs. Viktor Korchnoi chess game," 1.

the entire period—from Rollans' first move on 15 June 1985 to his last on (about) 14 February 1993.[159]

After noting that each chess move response from Rollans typically took about ten days, May asked: "Would this kind of protocol be accepted for a proof-of-principle laboratory experiment?"[160]

Since rigorous standards are expected from laboratory studies, similar rigor (specific to nonmaterialistic, non-scientific standards) *has* to be applied even for field studies that aim to provide proof-of-principle conclusions.[161]

Several comments are relevant here.

First of all, the possibility of fraud or hoax can never be *completely* ruled out in any field of study, *including laboratory studies*. There is *always* the logical possibility that fraud has occurred, and some lab researchers have indeed fudged their data. However, we do not need to completely exclude all logical possibility of fraud in order to draw conclusions whose validity we accept beyond reasonable doubt. With laboratory studies—which tend to be *much* simpler to deal with than field studies—we need independent replication. With field studies, we need only the independent emergence of other cases with the same characteristics. And as we have seen, there are indeed several such cases involving the display of high-level skills known to have been acquired by the departed but not by the medium, which have repeated themselves in several different contexts, and that come from the work of several different researchers.

159. May, "An alternative hypothesis for the Géza Maróczy (via medium Rollans) vs. Viktor Korchnoi chess game," 2.
160. May, "An alternative hypothesis for the Géza Maróczy (via medium Rollans) vs. Viktor Korchnoi chess game," 2.
161. May, "An alternative hypothesis for the Géza Maróczy (via medium Rollans) vs. Viktor Korchnoi chess game," 5.

Second, there remains the fact that knowledge can be gained outside of laboratory experiments, and that laboratory experiments are only suited to answer a very narrow range of questions. We do not need laboratory experiments under tightly controlled conditions to conclude that dinosaurs once roamed the planet, that the continents drift, or that rocks sometimes fall from the sky. Nor do we need laboratory experiments to be certain beyond reasonable doubt that Napoleon lost to Wellington at Waterloo, that Hitler committed suicide in Berlin, or that astronauts have walked on the moon.

In other words, laboratory experiments are not required to determine *that* something happened. Rather, laboratory experiments under tightly controlled conditions are required for accurately measuring *how* changes in an independent variable affect a dependent variable.

For instance, we may know beyond reasonable doubt that our friend was diagnosed with cancer, that he took an experimental new drug, and that now his cancer appears to be cured. But in order to more firmly support the conclusion that there is indeed a correlation between cancer survival rates and the new drug, laboratory experiments involving animal subjects with cancer need to be performed, under conditions as tightly controlled as possible. And note that once trials are begun on human subjects, then we are back to field studies, as no sane researcher would propose that the human subjects be kept in a laboratory setting under close watch twenty-four hours per day. Nor would anyone seriously propose *à la* May that the human subjects should be monitored by someone constantly at their side for months, or years.

And, as mentioned earlier, although we can be certain beyond reasonable doubt that a specific fact is true, we can never be certain beyond reasonable doubt that a scientific theory—which relates variables to each other—is true beyond reasonable doubt. The simple scientific theory "all swans are white" can never be proven true. But it can be proven false as soon as we are sure beyond reasonable doubt that this black bird before us really is a swan.

That extrasensory perception occurs has been accepted as fact in almost all cultures for thousands of years. Lab experiments are useful in determining the causal factors that influence the occurrence of ESP (such as relaxation, dreaming, emotional relationships, artistic ability, and so forth). Only with the rise of the philosophy of materialism in the eighteenth century did some educated people in the West raise ideological doubts against the very existence of ESP. In response, lab experiments were designed, not usually to discover causal factors, but in order to attempt the prove the very existence of ESP. When positive results were obtained again and again, "skeptics" did not change their minds. They demanded tighter and tighter controls, and even then they refused to accept the results. Their main tactic—then as now—is to demand proof beyond all conceivable doubt.

Most of the criticisms on the early ESP results focused on the possibility of fraud on the part of the subject, the experimenter, or both. The English psychologist C. E. M. Hansel wrote that "it is wise to adopt initially the assumption that ESP is impossible, since there is a great weight of knowledge supporting this point of view."[162] Hansel provided no documentation at all for this assumption. He merely went on to develop elaborate fraud scenarios to explain how each experiment could have been accomplished by fraud on the part of subject or experimenter.

---

162. Hansel, *ESP and Parapsychology*, 22.

In the 1930s, physiologist Joseph Banks Rhine set up the world's first university laboratory exclusively devoted to ESP research. Some of Rhine's most impressive results came from experiments with a student subject named Hubert Pearce. Preliminary experiments with specially designed cards seemed to indicate that Pearce had unusual psychic talents, and so Rhine was eager to devise a test for Pearce that would exclude every conceivable possibility of a normal explanation. He asked a research assistant named Gaither Pratt to perform a long-distance experiment, in which the subject, Pearce, located in one building, would attempt to identify the order of the cards as they were handled by Pratt, the experimenter, located in another building. In this way 1,850 trials were completed, resulting in 558 hits when only 370 would be expected by chance. The odds against these results occurring by chance were calculated to be astronomical, at 22 billion to one.

However, Hansel did not accept these results. He pointed out that Rhine and Pratt had failed to assign someone to watch Pearce at all times during the experiment. So it was *conceivable*, Hansel argued, that Pearce could have left the building he was in, made his way across campus to where Pratt was situated, peered through a glass window or through a trap door in the ceiling and spied on Pratt as he turned over the cards while compiling the target-sheet, completed his own target sheet, and then sneaked back to his station. Hansel never provided any evidence that fraud actually did occur; he merely raised the possibility that fraud *could have* occurred, and thereby argued that the experiments cannot be considered conclusive proof of ESP. Almost forty years after Rhine's classic work *ESP-60*, Hansel wrote:

A possible explanation other than [ESP], provided it involves only well-established processes, should not be rejected on the grounds of its complexity...If the result could have arisen through a trick, the experiment must be considered unsatisfactory proof of ESP, whether or not it is finally decided that such a trick was, in fact, used.[163]

His comments show the lengths a skeptic must be prepared to go in order to discount the early ESP experiments.

May is therefore no exception of a skeptic demanding proof beyond all conceivable doubt. There are really two problems with May's critique of the chess case: he offered nothing but pure speculation that Rollans committed fraud, and he criticized a field study on the impossible grounds that it did not employ laboratory-standard controls.

But, for all the reasons mentioned above, we have not a shred of evidence that Rollans masterminded an elaborate hoax, and plenty of reasons to believe that Rollans was not involved in any hoax. Hence, we may indeed conclude—beyond reasonable doubt only—that the facts of the case are as they seem. May is using the typical "skeptical" trick of attempting to create the illusion of reasonable doubt by demanding proof beyond all conceivable doubt, an impossible standard to meet when dealing with empirical matters. Wildly-speculative stories without a shred of supporting evidence do not constitute reasonable doubt. If May wishes to make an accusation of fraud, then, for all the reasons mentioned in Part I, the burden of proof is on him to provide supporting evidence. Abstract logical possibilities without a shred of supporting evidence do not raise reasonable doubt, only conceivable doubt.

The supposition that an elderly, frequently ill man with an impeccable reputation for honesty secretly conspired with a living chess master over seven years and eight months in order to mimic

---

163. Hansel, *ESP and Parapsychology*, 21.

the chess ability and style of a deceased grand master, and secretly travelled to Hungary to carry out an in-depth investigation of Maroczy's life, all for no apparent purpose or gain, and somehow did all of this without arousing the slightest suspicion of any of the five other persons directly involved,[164] can be safely rejected by all but the most dogmatic skeptics.

The only remaining explanation for this case—apart from genuine communication from Geza Maroczy—is that Rollans unconsciously used Super-ESP in order to pull off an elaborate fraud for no apparent purpose or gain. However, several features of this case create enormous difficulties for this hypothetical explanation.

Romi(h)

When Eisenbeiss questioned Maroczy about the life of Geza Maroczy, he at one point received a very unexpected answer. He asked Maroczy if he had ever known a player named Romi. Maroczy in reply mocked Eisenbeiss for not knowing the correct spelling, which Maroczy gave as "Romih." Eisenbeiss had no idea that name could be spelled that way.

Maroczy's answer was:

> I am sorry to say that I never knew a chess player named Romi. But I think you are wrong with the name. I had a friend in my youth, who defeated me when I was young, but he was called Romih—with an "h" at the end. I then never again saw the friend whom I so admired. In 1930 at the tournament of San Remo—who is also present? My old friend Romih coming from Italy also participated in that tournament. And so it came about that I played against him one of the most thrilling

---

164. Eisenbeiss, Schiebeler, Holbe, Korchnoi, and the historian-chess-player Sebestyén.

matches I ever played. I suspect that you were thinking about the same person but gave the name incorrectly.[165]

Which was the correct spelling? The Hungarian historian/chess player Sebestyén—who, as mentioned, was hired to find answers to the most obscure questions—found both spellings in the literature. Finally, a copy of the official book from the San Remo tournament of 1930 was found, with the spelling as "Romih." It turns out that after the 1930 tournament Romih moved to Italy and then dropped the *h*.

Eisenbeiss and Hassler concluded:

> Because *Maroczy* claimed to know Romih from his youth, it is logical that he would have known the original spelling of Romih's name and would not have replaced it with the later Italianization. For the Super-ESP Hypothesis to work, the controlling mind, on perceiving varying references to Romih or Romi, would have to be able to grasp the correct one from Maroczy's perspective, decide to address the situation, formulate a response to the conflict and dramatize it in the context of a teasing dialogue with Eisenbeiss/Rollans about their ignorance of the correct spelling.[166]

As Gauld would no doubt agree, we must be willing to attribute to Rollans not just Super-ESP, but super-artistry and super-*guile* as well.

The Vera Menchik Club

The August 4, 1988 edition of the Swiss chess magazine *Schachwoche* held a readers' competition, asking them: Who was the Austrian

---

165. Eisenbeiss and Hassler, "An Assessment of Ostensible Communications with a Deceased Grandmaster as Evidence for Survival," 74.

166. Eisenbeiss and Hassler, "An Assessment of Ostensible Communications with a Deceased Grandmaster as Evidence for Survival," 74–75.

founder of the Vera Menchik Club? Menchik was the first female world champion, and the club's members were those whom she had beaten.

Eisenbeiss asked Maroczy the same question on August 8, 1988. Maroczy confessed that he was uncertain and speculated on various names. He also describes the club as "a silly joke to which he paid no attention." On August 11, Maroczy considers Albert Becker as a possibility, but in the end rejects Becker. Note that the Super-ESP hypothesis would predict that the medium, posing as Maroczy, would give the correct name, because by August 4 the entire editing team at *Schachwoche* knew the correct name.

The solution was published in the same magazine on August 18, 1988: Albert Becker. On August 21, 1988, Maroczy is again asked for the founder's name. However:

> He still does not name Becker as the founder of the club, as might be expected under the Super-ESP hypothesis; once the solution was published it should be possible for the medium to access the information, either clairvoyantly, or telepathically from the minds of the magazine's readers. But instead of correcting his wrong answer *Maroczy* quite unprompted comes up with a different story which evidently demanded his attention much more than the "silly joke."[167]

Eisenbeis and Hassler concluded:

> In our example *Maroczy's* rationale for forgetting the name of a man whom he would have considered to be merely indulging a pointless joke but then relating an unprompted story about a woman whose beauty had impressed him is plausible, whereas for Rollans the medium it is difficult to understand [if using

---

167. Eisenbeiss and Hassler, "An Assessment of Ostensible Communications with a Deceased Grandmaster as Evidence for Survival," 76.

Super-ESP] why he should be unable to retrieve the name requested, given his ability to convey detailed precise information on other occasions, even less why he should digress to an umprompted narrative thread.[168]

The 1924 New York Tournament

A similar incident occurred when Maroczy was discussing a tournament in which he performed badly (by his standards). He discusses a "thrilling game" which he (correctly) says ended in a draw, but does not reveal his final ranking, admitting "it is true for me that I am not able to remember everything, most of all whenever winning eluded me."

Research revealed that Maroczy finished sixth in the tournament.

If Rollans were trying to engineer a story with verifiable facts as evidence of survival, he could have inserted Maroczy's final ranking, a checkable fact. Clearly, elsewhere the Maroczy transcripts contain innumerable such verifiable facts...we know Maroczy to have been very ambitious and it is thus entirely in character that he would omit reporting failures or mediocre tournament rankings. Yet for Rollans, whose main objective was to provide convincing evidence to support the survival hypothesis, it would make no sense to censor information concerning Maroczy's failures.[169]

Discussion

What is so impressive about this case is the demonstration of a high-level skill (knowing *how*) combined with near-perfect accuracy in answers to questions about an obscure life in the early

---

168. Eisenbeiss and Hassler, "An Assessment of Ostensible Communications with a Deceased Grandmaster as Evidence for Survival," 80. And note the similarity to the medium's failure to recognize Miss Warner in the case involving George Pellew, despite the fact that sources for telepathy and clairvoyance were also readily on hand (see chapter 9).

169. Eisenbeiss and Hassler, "An Assessment of Ostensible Communications with a Deceased Grandmaster as Evidence for Survival," 77, 78, 80.

twentieth century (knowing *that*), and all presented in the style and from the perspective of a deceased grand master.

Neppe describes the difficulty of using any form of ESP to explain the chess-playing skill attributed to Maroczy:

> Far more so, chess-playing skill requires a further profound leap when applying the super-ESP hypothesis—delving into a Master's (or several Master's) *unconscious* mind(s) is insufficient; their *active repeated cogitation* 47 times (as 47 moves) over many years plus the medium obtaining it all by automatic writing... Merely divining this information from the Master's unconscious would not work, as the responses would require active intervention.[170]

In other words, much more than mere *perception* is required: also required is the *active thinking* of the mind of at least one chess master, living or departed. And, as we have seen, Super-ESP utterly fails to explain not just one but *four* features of this remarkable case.

Implication of Skills for ESP

Demonstration of high-level skills known to be possessed by a deceased communicator, but not possessed by the medium, is even more difficult to explain via any form of extrasensory perception than the convincing impersonation of someone the medium has never met (or closely studied on film). This is because studies show that top-level performers *always* require many years of hard practice before achieving excellence.

Journalist Geoff Colvin has noted:

---

170. Neppe, "A Detailed Analysis of an Important Chess Game," 146–147.

In a famous study of chess players, Nobel Prize winner Herbert Simon and Willian Chase proposed the "ten-year rule," based on their observation that no one seemed to reach the top ranks of chess players without a decade or so of intensive study, and some required much more time. Even [child prodigy] Bobby Fischer was not an exception; when he became a grand master at age sixteen, he had been studying chess intensively for nine years. Subsequent research in a wide range of fields has substantiated the ten-year rule everywhere the researchers have looked. In math, science, musical composition, swimming, X-ray diagnosis, tennis, literature—no one, not even the most "talented" performers, became great without at least ten years of very hard preparation.[171]

There is therefore no reason at all to assume that mere *perception*—extrasensory or otherwise—can enable anyone to instantly and temporarily acquire skills normally requiring years of practice to acquire.

So far, we have seen that Super-ESP was first proposed when the hypothesis of telepathy between medium and sitter was proven false by the continued success of proxy sittings. The hard-core materialists were left with no alternative other than the speculation of vast, virtually unlimited powers of ESP, enabling the medium to instantly and telepathically retrieve information from the minds of strangers, regardless of what those strangers may have been thinking about at the time, and to instantly and clairvoyantly retrieve information from written documents, regardless of whether the medium knows of the existence of those documents. And Super-ESP by itself was not enough: also required was the *unconscious deception* of the medium, pretending to be the deceased.

---

171. Colvin, *Talent is Overrated*, 61–61.

Analysis of other cases revealed that even this was not enough. The medium also needed to cunningly—and unconsciously—employ super-*artistry* and super-*guile* in order to adopt the *purpose* and *perspective* unique to the deceased. Finally, the Super-ESP hypothesis needs to be stretched even further, as the medium must not only unconsciously employ vast abilities of extrasensory perception, super-artistry, and super-guile: the Super-ESP hypothesis also requires the *ad hoc* addition of skills that have nothing to do with *any form of perception*, extrasensory or otherwise. Now we are asked to assume—without a shred of supporting evidence—that the medium can use extrasensory perception to brilliantly impersonate deceased individuals she did not or barely knew, and can also use telepathy and clairvoyance to *instantly* and *temporarily* acquire the skills that required those same deceased individuals years of practice to acquire during their time on Earth.

Commenting on such cases, Broad wrote,

> It seems to me that any attempt to explain these phenomena by reference to telepathy among the living stretches the word "telepathy" till it becomes almost meaningless, and uses that name to cover something for which there is no *independent* evidence and which bears hardly any analogy to the phenomena which the word was introduced to denote.[172]

In other words, whenever the hypothesis of living-agent ESP was falsified by the data, it was simply extended with speculative, untestable auxiliary assumptions that have nothing to do with extrasensory perception as the term is normally understood.

And even these *ad hoc* additions are not enough.

---

172. Broad, *Lectures on Psychical Research*, 427. The word *telepathy* is derived from the Greek words *tele* meaning "distant" and *pathy* meaning "feeling." So *telepathy* literally means "distant feeling."

Chapter 11
Evidence of Design

Frederic Myers, whom we met earlier as one of the founding members of the British Society for Psychical Research, died on January 17, 1901. During his life he had been a classical scholar, extremely well versed in the literature and poetry of ancient Greece and Rome. Myers had been intensely interested in the survival problem, and had spent a great deal of time and effort investigating the evidence. However, although he himself came to believe in survival, Myers was also fully aware of the difficulty of finding evidence that could not be explained by determined skeptics as due to some form of superpowerful ESP combined with unconscious deception.

The problem is this: most of the evidence for survival coming from mediums consists of communications of knowledge not known to anyone present, but that was, or could very well have been, known to the deceased. Now it is clear that if such communications are to be of any value as evidence, then the information conveyed must be capable of being verified; and this implies that some living person or persons must know the facts, or that some written record of them exists somewhere. But if the knowledge is recorded—either in memories of the living or in writing—then it is always possible, at least in principle, that the knowledge was gained from the telepathic or clairvoyant powers of the medium.

As mentioned, Myers was fully aware of this problem. What makes the cross correspondences so unusual is that they appear to be a method invented by the postmortem Myers in order to overcome this difficulty. In other words, they appear to be a method invented to provide evidence of his survival, which would be very difficult—if not impossible—to explain on the basis of telepathy or clairvoyance among the living.

The messages that became known as the cross correspondences were received by mediums in England, the United States, and India, during the period 1901 to 1932. Their distinguishing feature is that they appear to be meaningless when read by themselves. But when combined with messages received by other mediums at about the same time, they show various correspondences, so that when a group of them is considered together, they clearly refer to some common topic, usually from classical literature or history. They are in the form of literary puzzles, analogous to the pieces of a crossword puzzle—individually meaningless, but when combined form a pattern. The nature of these puzzles seems to rule out telepathy between the mediums as their source. After all, if each medium does not understand their own part of the message, then how could they transmit the corresponding messages that complete and solve the puzzle?

A further difficulty these puzzles raise for the hypothesis of telepathy is that many of them required knowledge of the classics that far exceeded the knowledge of most of the mediums involved—but not that of the living Myers. In some of the best cases, solving the puzzles required a great deal of study on the part of the investigators. And throughout these investigations, the mediums frequently remained ignorant of what the other automatists had written.

Shortly after Myers died, messages purporting to come from him were received by several mediums in different parts of the world. Most of these messages were received by the technique of automatic writing, in which the medium enters a trance and writes with pencil or pen on paper. Many of these messages expressed a passionate longing to establish his survival. For instance, after his death Mrs. Holland in India wrote in trance: "If it were possible for the soul to die back into earth life I should die from sheer yearning to reach you to tell you that all we imagined is not half wonderful enough for the truth." And through Mrs. Piper in Boston: "I am trying with all the forces together to prove that I am Myers."[173]

But other messages received through various mediums throughout the world, also signed "Myers," were cryptic literary allusions; it seemed as though their true meanings were being deliberately concealed. As according to SPR protocol, the messages were sent to Miss Alice Johnson of the BSPR, and it was not until early 1906 that she realized what was happening. By that time the scripts contained the astounding claim that the deceased Myers had devised a scheme of providing meaningless fragments in the scripts of different mediums, fragments which would be found to express a coherent idea only when combined.

There are many passages in the scripts that bear this out. The automatists are exhorted "to weave together" and are told that by themselves they can do little. In the script of Mrs. Verrall, we find, "Record the bits and when fitted they will make the whole," and, "I will give the words between you neither alone can read but together they will give the clue he wants."[174] It is constantly claimed

173. Saltmarsh, *Evidence of Personal Survival from Cross Correspondences*, 31.
174. Saltmarsh, *Evidence of Personal Survival from Cross Correspondences*, 36.

in the scripts that the enigmatic messages are part of an experiment designed to provide convincing evidence of survival, and that the source of the enigmatic messages is the mind of Frederic Myers; or later, of some of his deceased colleagues.

The quest to solve the puzzle of the *cross correspondences* had begun. As mentioned, the messages received via various mediums in various parts of the world were sent, according to SPR protocol, to Miss Alice Johnson of the BSPR, and it was the highly analytical Miss Johnson who first realized what was happening. In her article of 1908, the theory of the cross correspondences is fully discussed for the first time. She first described the nature of the messages:

> What we get is fragmentary utterance in one script, which seems to have no particular point or meaning, and another fragmentary utterance in the other, of an equally pointless character; but when we put the two together, we see that they supplement one another, and that there is apparently one coherent idea underlying both, but only partially expressed in each.

Miss Johnson then described the apparent origin of the messages:

> Now, granted the possibility of communication, it may be supposed that within the last few years a certain group of persons have been trying to communicate with us, who are sufficiently well instructed to know all the objections that reasonable sceptics have urged against the previous evidence, and sufficiently intelligent to realize the full force of these objections. It may be supposed that these persons have invented a new plan—the plan of cross-correspondences—to meet the sceptic's objection …

> We have reason to believe … that the idea of making a statement in one script *complementary* of a statement in another had not occurred to Mr. Myers in his lifetime, for there is no reference to it in any of his written utterances on the subject that I have been able to discover … It was not the autonomists that

detected it, but a student of the scripts; it has every appearance of being an element imported from outside; it suggests an independent invention, an active intelligence constantly at work in the present, not a mere echo or remnant of individualities of the past.[175]

What the cross correspondences add to the evidence from mediumship is *evidence of design*—a design that could not have originated in the minds of anyone living, but which gives every indication of being designed by the mind of Frederic Myers.

There is not space here to deal with the cross correspondences in the depth they deserve.[176] However, the following description of one case, taken from my third book, is a useful illustration. Note that, as was the case with several of the mediums involved in the cross correspondences, both women were well-respected public figures who kept their mediumship a closely guarded secret. Mrs. Verrall was a lecturer at Cambridge, England; Mrs. Holland was the pseudonym of Mrs. Fleming, a sister of Rudyard Kipling, and she lived in India.

The Roden Noel Case

On March 7, 1906, Mrs. Verrall's script contained an original poem, which started with the words:

Tintagel and the sea that moaned in pain.

When Miss Johnson read this she was struck by its similarity to a poem by Roden Noel, entitled "Tintagel."[177] To the best of her recollection, Mrs. Verrall had never read this poem.

---

175. Saltmarsh, *Evidence of Personal Survival from Cross Correspondences*, 36–7.
176. An excellent analysis of these cases can be found in the book by Saltmarsh listed in the bibliography. Also see chapters 14–16 in my third book *Science and the Afterlife*.
177. The first two lines of the poem are: *Tintagel, from thy precipice of rock / Thou frown back the vast Atlantic shock.*

On March 11, 1906, Mrs. Holland's script contained these words:

> "This is for A. W. Ask him what the date May 26th, 1894, meant to him—to me—and to F. W. H. M. I do not think they will find it hard to recall, but if so—let them ask Nora."

The date given, which meant nothing to Mrs. Holland, is the death of Roden Noel. The initials A. W. refer to professor A. W. Verrall, and F. W. H. M. refers of course to F. W. H. Myers, both of whom knew Noel, but not very well. Nora means Mrs. Sidgwick, which seems appropriate, as Noel was an intimate friend of Dr. Sidgwick.

On March 14, before any of the above facts were known to Mrs. Holland, she wrote in a trance state:

> Eighteen, fifteen, four, five, fourteen, fourteen, fifteen, five, twelve. Not to be taken as they stand. See Rev. 13, 18, but only the central eight words, not the whole passage.[178]

The whole thing was meaningless to Mrs. Holland, and she did not look up the passage. But Miss Johnson did, and found that the central eight words were *for it is the number of a man*. Taking this to be a hint, she translated the numbers given in the script into the letters of the alphabet, with *d* being the fourth letter, *e* the fifth, and so on. When finished, the letters spelled *Roden Noel*.

There was a further reference to Roden Noel in Mrs. Verrall's script of March 16, 1906, and finally, on March 28, 1906, Mrs. Holland's script contained the name *Roden Noel* written out in full. Hence, the common topic of the scripts was only revealed in a later script, and by the dutiful efforts of Miss Johnson to understand the earlier scripts.

---

178. Quoted in Saltmarsh, *Evidence of Personal Survival from Cross Correspondences,* 57.

Comments on the Roden Noel Case

In this cross correspondence between two mediums, we find three references to the same person but given in an indirect manner, which did not reveal the chosen topic to the conscious minds of the mediums. This deliberate concealment seems to be crucial to the plan of the cross correspondences: the messages are deliberately enigmatic to prevent the mediums from acquiring knowledge of the topic, in order to rule out the possibility of the mediums helping each other, normally or telepathically.[179]

To sum up the case so far: in order to deal with the cross correspondences, the Super-ESP hypothesis must be stretched even further. At this point the "skeptic" must ask us to seriously entertain, without a single shred of evidence, the possibility that the unconscious minds of *several* mediums in different parts of the world are able to use Super-ESP to simultaneously coordinate elaborate, *unconscious plots of deception*. And if the plots are carried out unconsciously, then how could we ever find any evidence, for or against?

We will now see that even this desperate, untestable *ad hoc* addition is not enough to rescue Super-ESP.

---

179. Carter, *Science and the Afterlife*, 230-1.

Chapter 12
Mental Characteristics Only of the Deceased

The death of Mrs. Verrall in 1916 made very little difference to the content of the cross correspondence scripts. This contrasts sharply with the change in the scripts following the death of her husband, Dr. A. W. Verrall, on June 18, 1912. Within a few weeks of his death messages purportedly from Verrall began to appear, these also in the form of enigmatic literary puzzles. When solved, they too revealed themselves as requiring specialized knowledge of the classics possessed by very few living scholars, but known to be possessed by the living Verrall.[180]

Earlier, we saw that the accompanying messages also displayed many idiosyncratic personality characteristics of the living Verrall, which led three people—an intimate friend of Verrall's, his surviving wife, and a niece—to agree with his old friend Bayfield's assessment, that "to me at least it is incredible that even the cleverest could achieve such an unexampled triumph in deceptive impersonation as this would be if the actor is not Verrall himself."

---

180. Excellent summaries of these cases can be found in Saltmarsh, *Evidence of Personal Survival from Cross Correspondences*, chapter VI.

The Lethe Experiment

The final case we will consider began on March 23, 1908, when Mr. G. B. Dorr, a member of the SPR, posed the following question to "Myers" through the medium Mrs. Piper in Boston: "What does the word *Lethe* suggest to you?" In Greek mythology, River Lethe flows through Hades, and is also known as the River of Forgetfulness. The dead are said to drink from this river to obliterate their memories, before being born again on Earth. Dorr was expecting a reply along these lines. Instead, he got the following strange answer:

MYERS: Lethe. Do you refer to one of my poems, Lethe?

Dorr answered in the negative, and pressed the communicator for another answer. But instead of getting the answer he expected, he received a disjointed reply that included references to a cave, to winds, to "entwined love," and to an arrow shot through the air. None of this made any sense to Dorr.

At another sitting the next day with Mrs. Piper, communicators claiming to be Hodgson and Myers came through, and both clearly expressed concern that Dorr did not understand the previous day's answer.

HODGSON: Now Myers feels a little distressed because he thinks you did not quite understand his replies to your last question [i.e., the question about Lethe].

DORR: I ought not to have brought any questions up after the letters and the talk they led to. [The early part of the seance the day before was concerned with letters Dorr read to "Myers."]

HODGSON: No, quite right, but he did give you one or two replies which he and I both fear you did not understand.

DORR: No, it wasn't clear. I worked over the sittings yesterday till nearly midnight, trying to straighten things out.

HODGSON: Let Myers explain what he thinks you did not grasp.

MYERS: I wrote in reply to your last inquiry Cave—Lethe.

DORR: I asked him [i.e., Myers] whether the word *Lethe* recalled anything to him.

HODGSON: He replied Cave—Banks—Shore … He drew the form—a picture of Iris with an arrow.

DORR: But he spoke of winds.

MYERS: Yes, clouds—arrow—Iris—Cave—Mor MOR Latin for sleep *Morpheus—Cave.* Sticks in my mind can't you help me?

DORR: Good. I understand what you are after now. But can't you make it clearer about what there was peculiar about the waters of Lethe?

MYERS: Yes, I suppose you think that I am affected in the same way *but I am not.*[181]

It is worth noting here that the major investigator of this case, Piddington, commented on the last line above as follows: "The way in which Myers here withheld the obvious and commonplace answer until pressed to give it by Mr. Dorr is, I think, deserving of the utmost attention; for this avoidance of the trite and obvious creates a presumption that Myers deliberately preferred so to frame his messages that only study and thought would render them intelligible."[182]

Later in this sitting, and in the next a few days later, the following came through:

I walked in the garden of the gods—entranced I stood along its banks—like one entranced I saw her at last … Elysian shores.

181. Piddington, "Three Incidents from the Sittings," 90–91.
182. Piddington, "Three Incidents from the Sittings," 91.

We walk together, our loves entwined, along the shores. In beauty beyond comparison with Lethe. Sorry it is all so fragmentary but suppose it cannot all get through.

Orpheus and Eurydice. It reminds me of them.[183]

In seances over the following days, various references to names in classical literature are made, and Dorr found four authors from antiquity in whose work appear these names. In a subsequent seance, Dorr mentioned three of these names to the communicator: Aristophanes, Horace, and Ovid, to which "Myers" replied:

I remember well OVID.[184]

This was the clue that led to the eventual solution to this puzzle.

Comments on This Case

The investigators, several of whom were classical scholars, were at first utterly perplexed by these messages. Piddington, who eventually became the lead investigator of this case, was impressed by the confidence expressed in the messages that they were indeed relevant to the original question, and after following up on some clues in the messages, noted how he "by good luck came on a passage in the eleventh book, hitherto unknown to me, of the *Metamorphoses* of Ovid, which explains and justifies the main part of the answers given in the trance."[185]

In my chapter-long review of this case, I described the conclusion eventually reached by the investigators:

---

183. Piddington, "Three Incidents from the Sittings," 105.
184. Piddington, "Three Incidents from the Sittings," 114.
185. Piddington, "Three Incidents from the Sittings," 98–9.

This puzzle shows evidence of a design that was not at all apparent to any of the investigators, but it is a design that the living Myers was certainly capable of creating. The design required detailed knowledge of Ovid which Mrs. Piper and the others simply did not possess. The associations provided in the script were ones Myers would have naturally made, but associations that at first left Mrs. Piper, Dorr, Mrs. Verrall, Lord Balfour, Piddington, and the other investigators completely baffled.[186]

There are also personal touches in the scripts that point to the distinctive personality and interests of Frederic Myers. Classical references appear to both Ovid and Virgil, both of whom were objects of special admiration to Myers. Also, three stories in Ovid's *Metamorphoses X* are alluded to in the three successive scripts, and Piddington discovered that the order in which the allusions emerge in the scripts is *not* the order in which they appear in *Metamorphoses*, but they are the order in which they appear in one of Myers's poems.

The references to Orpheus and Eurydice—lovers reunited in another realm—was a theme very near to Myers's heart and appears in several of his poems. At age thirty Myers fell in love with a married woman who died three years later.

And this is not all there is to this remarkable case.

Lodge Continues the Experiment

At the time Dorr was questioning Mrs. Piper in Boston, Sir Oliver Lodge was also in Boston, and thought it would be useful to test the "Myers" communicator by asking the same question of Mrs. Willett in England. So, in a letter, to be read to Mrs. Willett, he wrote: "What does the word *Lethe* suggest to you?" Note that Mrs.

---

186. Carter, *Science and the Afterlife*, 243.

Willett in England had no normal knowledge of the question that was asked through Mrs. Piper in Boston.

On February 4, 1910, Mrs. Willett in trance wrote, "Myers yes I am here," and the question was read. The script began at once.

> *Myers the will again to live*
> *the River of forgetfulness*

And later in the script, after several classical references to River Lethe, these lines appeared:

> *there was a door to which I found no key*
> *and Haggi Babba too*
> *This is disconnected but not meaningless*

This was followed by further various classical references to Lethe, and the script ended with "enough for to-day Myers."[187]

The next day Mrs. Willett suddenly felt an overpowering urge to write, sat down, and wrote:

> You felt the call … it is I who write Myers I need urgently to say this tell Lodge this word … the word is DORR.

The allusions to Lethe in the script of February 4 are obvious. The first sentence, "The will again to live," is from a poem written by the living Myers, and refers to souls gathering on the banks of Lethe, waiting to drink the waters of forgetfulness, and willing again to live on Earth.[188]

> *God the innumerous souls in great array*
> *To Lethe summons by a wondrous way*

---

187. Lodge, "Evidence of Classical Scholarship and of Cross-correspondence in Some New Automatic Writings," 117.

188. Lodge, "Evidence of Classical Scholarship and of Cross-Correspondence in Some New Automatic Writings," 132.

> *Till these therein their ancient pain forgive*
> *Forget their life, and will again to live*

Recall that the *first response* of Mrs. Piper's Myers communicator in response to the Lethe question had been: "Do you refer to one of my poems?" This answer was thought by both Dorr and Piddington to be confused and inappropriate; Piddington had at first failed to discover any mention of Lethe in any of Frederic Myers original poems.[189]

Abruptly at one point the subject is changed, and a quote from the Persian poet Omar Khayyam is given: "There was a door to which I found no key," followed by what seems to be an attempt at the name Ali Babba of *Ali Babba and the Forty Thieves*, and by the words, "This is disconnected but not meaningless."

On March 7 the Myers communicator wrote, "There was a pun but I do not want to say where." Lodge searched the script for a pun, and on June 5 he told "Myers" through Mrs. Willett that he could not find any pun. In response, the entranced Mrs. Willett wrote:

Re LETHE … I, Myers, made a pun, I got in a word I wanted by wrapping it in a QUOTATION. Later I got the WORD itself.

Sir Oliver interpreted this as referring to the word *door* in the Omar Khayyam quotation as a pun on the name Dorr, the American who first asked Myers the question about Lethe through Mrs. Piper. The door to the robber's cave in the Ali Babba story only opened with the words *Open Sesame*, which could be described as "a door to which I found no key." The fact that the name Dorr was given spontaneously the following day seems to justify this interpretation.

The Myers communicator evidently understood what Dorr and Lodge were trying to accomplish, for in a script on February 10

---

189. Piddington, "Three Incidents from the Sittings," 87.

(five days after he first mentioned the word *DORR* in the script of Mrs. Willet) he wrote, "Dorr's scheme excellent. That I have different scribes means that I must show different aspects of thoughts underlying which unity is to be found," and, "I know what Lodge wants. He wants me to prove that I have access to knowledge shown elsewhere."[190]

As mentioned at the beginning of Part II, the emphasis here has been on *why* the very best cases for survival are so compelling. As such, it is not fitting to include in this book the entire number of impressive features of this case that indicate only the mind of Frederic Myers could have been the author of the messages received on both sides of the Atlantic. Those readers interested in a more exhaustive review of this case may consult my third book *Science and the Afterlife*.

However, even without reviewing this entire case in detail, we have more than enough information to conclude that this case is virtually impossible to explain away as the work of living-agent ESP.

Stated simply, the defender of the ESP hypothesis has to explain not only how telepathy—as the term is normally understood—was employed by a woman almost completely unfamiliar with the classics in order to *instantly* track down obscure classical references, from sources with which she had no personal connection. The defender must also explain how the associations specifically chosen from the classics were those that *only Myers* might have made with the name *Lethe*. In his review of the cross correspondences, Saltmarsh noted the implications these associations have for establishing personal identity:

---

190. Saltmarsh, *Evidence of Personal Survival from Cross Correspondences*, 95–6. See also Lodge, "Evidence of Classical Scholarship and of Cross-Correspondence in Some New Automatic Writings."

Some of the most characteristic individual possessions of the human mind are the associations which it makes between ideas. These associations are the result of past history and are as clear an indication of psychical individuality as finger-prints are of physical. No two persons will make exactly the same associations between ideas, because no two persons have ever exactly the same history.[191]

The answers given to the Lethe question appear to have been deliberately chosen so that they would not be initially understood by the investigators; however, after a great deal of detailed investigation, they were found to have all the hallmarks of Myers's unique interests, personality, and classical education. As Ducasse pointed out,

To account for such an ingenious feat of inventive and constructive activity as the purported Myers performed in this case, something different from ESP *in kind*, not just in degree, is indispensable; namely, either Myers's own mind at work, or else a duplicate of it; which, however, then needs to be itself accounted for.[192]

In a 1908 review of some of the earliest cross correspondences, Piddington wrote:

The only opinion which I hold with confidence is this: that if it was not the mind of Frederic Myers it was one which deliberately and artistically imitated his mental characteristics.[193]

Piddington disliked the idea of survival, and yet as the years passed, he was driven more and more to the conclusion that communication from the surviving minds of Myers, Verrall, and the

---

191. Saltmarsh, *Evidence of Personal Survival from Cross Correspondences*, 134.
192. Ducasse, "What Would Constitute Conclusive Evidence of Survival after Death?" 406.
193. Piddington, "A Series of Concordant Automisms," 243.

others was the most plausible explanation for the cross correspondences. With very few exceptions, the other SPR investigators came to the same conclusion.

The Super-ESP hypothesis attempts to explain the seeming communication from the departed as due to telepathy and clairvoyance among the living. But as Ducasse remarked:

> When Occam's razor is alleged to shave off survival as a superfluous hypothesis, and to leave ESP as sufficient to account for all the facts in evidence, it turns out that ESP cannot do it without being arbitrarily endowed with an *ad hoc* "beard" consisting not of capacity for more far-reaching perception, but of capacity for reasoning, inventing, constructing, understanding, judging; i.e., for *active thinking*; and more specifically, for the particular modes of such active thinking which *only* the particular mind whose survival is in question is *known* to have been equipped with.[194]

And so, it should be clear at this point that the crucial difference between the best mediumship cases and extrasensory perception involving only the living is this: *the active participation of the departed person's mind* seems to be required, not just merely the gathering of information *about* the departed person's life.

---

194. Ducasse, "What would Constitute Conclusive Evidence of Survival after Death?" 405.

Part III
RIP Super-ESP

We have seen that extrasensory perception among the living—whether super or otherwise—is incapable of explaining the very best cases for survival, from five independent lines of evidence. Now, we will consider some final points, in the light of all that we have covered. Chapter 13 asks if there is any evidence that Super-ESP even exists; chapter 14 considers the arguments of philosopher Stephen Braude; last, we bring everything together, and we arrive at a final conclusion.

Chapter 13
Does Super-ESP Exist?

Extrasensory perception includes the following abilities: *telepathy*, Greek for "distant feeling"; and *clairvoyance*, French for "clear vision."

Both abilities have been convincingly and independently demonstrated under controlled conditions in laboratories around the world. The most convincing evidence for telepathy comes from the *Ganzfeld* experiments, in which one person, called the sender, concentrates on a picture, called the target. In another room is the receiver whose role is to relax and let images and thoughts come into their mind. After thirty minutes of concentration on the target by the sender, and of open relaxation on the part of the receiver, the session ends and the receiver is shown four pictures and asked to choose the one seen by the sender. By sheer chance, they should be right about 25 percent of the time; but results show an average accuracy rate of about 33 percent. Although some of the most gifted subjects show an accuracy rate exceeding 50 percent, *nothing* in the Ganzfeld suggests that messages of any sort may be sent and received via telepathy, and certainly nothing in the Ganzfeld suggests that articulate, real-time conversations may be held between participants, of the sort that we have seen in several of the mediumship cases covered earlier. Nothing displayed in the Ganzfeld comes even remotely close to being powerful enough to explain away the survival evidence.

The common reply by defenders of Super-ESP is that extrasensory perception in real life, "in the wild," may be much more impressive than that typically found in labs. This may seem plausible, as the evidence indicates that the use of extrasensory perception in real life is goal oriented, operating to serve some purpose for the person or animal, as opposed to merely satisfying a lab researcher's desire to publish favorable results in an academic journal. However, even in the wild, the evidence indicates that ESP includes little more than a very low-level set of abilities: most reports of ESP in real life are no more impressive than a sense of being stared at, or of anticipating a phone call from a friend or relative.[195]

Philosopher Stephen Braude, whom we will meet in the next chapter, is strangely unbothered by the utter lack of evidence for Super-ESP or super versions of *psi* (a blanket term referring to extrasensory perception plus psychokinesis): "Widespread, large scale and inconspicuous *psi* would be the sort of phenomenon whose existence might never be conclusively demonstrated or disproved."[196] It should be immediately obvious that when stated in these terms, the possible existence of Super-ESP "whose existence might never be conclusively demonstrated or disproved" has the same logical status as Descartes's evil demon theory—that an all-powerful demon created the world and us, complete with our memories, only five minutes ago. Or, using a more modern take on this idea, it has the same logical status as the imaginary possi-

---

195. See Sheldrake, *The Sense of Being Stared At*.
196. Braude, "Evaluating the Super-psi Hypothesis," 35.

bility that we live in a computer-simulated dream world, as popularized in the science-fiction film *The Matrix*. All three ideas are among a virtually infinite number of unfalsifiable fantasies that are without any shred of supporting evidence, meaning of course that no sane person should seriously entertain any of them as real possibilities. And note the contradiction implicit in the description of Super-psi as possibly being "widespread, large scale and inconspicuous": if extrasensory perception and psychokinesis were indeed widespread and large scale, then how could they also possibly remain *inconspicuous*?

Logical consistency aside, do we have any reason to believe that wild ESP is at least capable of explaining the remarkable provision of accurate information that we so often find in the survival evidence?

If the function of Super-ESP is the use of its virtually unlimited powers by the subconscious mind to surreptitiously protect us from the abstract fear of death by fabricating elaborate evidence that seems in every respect exactly *as if* the deceased are visiting or communicating, then why don't we have evidence of our unconscious minds employing these vast powers to protect us from the *actual* threat of imminent death? That would at least provide a more plausible evolutionary reason for the existence of these powers.

The theory of the unconscious employment of vast powers of ESP would therefore seem to predict that these powers should, at least occasionally, be used to save us not from merely the abstract fear of death, but from actual imminent death. Plenty of potential opportunities can be found in history. Consider the various tragic wars of the twentieth century. Surely there must have been many occasions in which captured soldiers could have saved themselves from death or incarceration by instantly acquiring the ability to speak a foreign language fluently and thus passing themselves off as compatriots. Answering test questions such as "Which city is the capital of … ?" would seem child's play compared to the vast powers of telepathy and clairvoyance the proponents of Super-ESP attribute to mediums.

But we have not one single shred of evidence that unfortunate people on either side of any conflict were able to save themselves from death or lengthy and brutal incarceration by using these vast hypothetical powers. And if the proponents of Super-ESP argue that these abilities only become manifest in a trance state, then we may wonder why trance mediums in heavily bombed London were not invaluable guides to German plans and intentions. The only example I have found of a medium being usefully employed by British Intelligence is Geraldine Cummins, but the information she supplied invariably seemed to come from deceased individuals, and gave no indication of omniscient Super-ESP.[197] But in 1944 the medium Helen Duncan was charged and convicted of witchcraft (!) because she provided relatives with messages from deceased sailors regarding the sinking of their ships, which British High Command wished to keep secret for fear of harming public morale.[198] Plenty of other examples can easily be found from WWII in which people could have reduced not merely the abstract fear of death but the threat of actual imminent death by the employment of the vast, virtually unlimited telepathic and clairvoyant powers attributed to mediums by the proponents of Super-ESP.

Having said this, there are in fact accounts from the Second World War of people using psychic abilities to save their lives. One of the most famous involved Winston Churchill, whose life was saved during a bombing raid on London by a *feeling* that he should

197. See Cousins, "Writer, Medium, Suffragette, Spy?"
198. See Crossley, *The Story of Helen Duncan*.

not sit in his usual place in his staff car. Rupert Sheldrake reports the case of a British soldier in Malaya who *felt* he was being stared at, accompanied by an acute sense of danger. Upon turning, he saw an enemy soldier about twenty yards away, bringing up his rifle to fire. The British soldier shot first, killing his enemy and thereby saving his own life.[199] These and other historical accounts do not stretch the original meaning of the words *telepathy* ("distant feeling") or *clairvoyance* ("clear vision"), and are described in detail in my first book.

---

199. Sheldrake, *The Sense of Being Stared At*, xii.

Chapter 14

The Arguments of Stephen Braude

The hypothesis of Super-ESP as a counterexplanation for the survival evidence has been vigorously defended by philosopher Stephen Braude, whose starting point is essentially this: although we have good evidence for the existence of extrasensory perception (ESP) and psychokinesis (PK), at present, we do not know the limits of ESP. As Braude frequently asserts in various ways, "Just as we have no grounds at present for assuming that PK has any limits at all, the same is no doubt true with regard to the forms of ESP,"[200] and, "Disheartening as it may be, we simply have no decent idea what (if any) magnitude of phenomena is implausible or unlikely, once we have allowed psi to occur at all."[201]

So far, so good: we do not currently know the limits of extrasensory perception. But Braude then goes further, and argues that ruling out ESP as an explanation of the data for survival *assumes unjustifiably* that ESP has limits that we can specify in advance.

---

200. Braude, *The Limits of Influence*, 196.
201. Braude, *The Limits of Influence*, 196.

The philosopher Robert Almeder has thoroughly examined Braude's arguments on Super-ESP, and he agrees that no one should place any *a priori* limits on ESP or psi (as mentioned, extra-sensory perception and psychokinesis lumped together are called *psi*, pronounced *sigh*).

> However, it seems reasonable to point out that, before one can appeal legitimately to super-ESP as an alternative way of explaining anything, one should have some empirical evidence that in fact super-ESP exists. This evidence is not provided simply by noting that it is possible—logically possible—that such super-ESP exists. [Those] who reject super-ESP explanations do so, presumably, because they think the burden of proof should be on the proponents of super-ESP to provide evidence for its existence if the appeal to it is to serve as an alternative explanation for an existing body of data. Insisting that super-ESP be empirically confirmed to exist before it may be used to explain anything seems less an instance of assuming erroneously that there are a priori limits to ESP than simply just that: a request for some evidence of the causes cited in offering an explanation. Jones could hardly be the robber of the Rabun Gap Bank if we have no good reason to think that Jones ever existed.[202]

And note that even *if* it could be demonstrated that some form of super-powerful ESP does exist in some limited cases, evidence must be shown that it explains *the specific case under consideration*. A useful analogy would be a criminal trial in which the defense argues that we cannot rule out police corruption as an explanation for the evidence, on the ground that we do not know the limits of police corruption. The correct reply is of course that while we may not know the limits of police corruption—such as how far

---

202. Almeder, *Death & Personal Survival*, 52.

it goes up the ranks—we may still demand positive evidence of alleged corruption in this specific case. Objecting that we have no evidence of corruption in this case is not to place any arbitrary limits on police corruption, but rather to ask two simple questions: (1) Is there any evidence of police corruption in this case? (2) Are there reasons to believe that police corruption *cannot* explain all the facts in this case? Asking these questions in no way arbitrarily assumes there are some *a priori* limits to the extent of corruption within the department.

With regard to the second point, the prosecutor may go even further and demonstrate reasons why police corruption cannot explain certain features of the case currently in trial. We may not know the actual limits of police corruption, but we do have good reasons to believe that corruption, to whatever extent it may or may not exist, is simply not *capable* of certain accomplishments. For instance, we have no reason to believe that corrupt police officers are capable of implanting false memories in the minds of witnesses. Nor do we have any reason to believe that the use of any form of perception, extrasensory or otherwise, can enable anyone to convincingly impersonate someone they have never met, and to instantly acquire their hard-earned skills.

And we have seen several features in cases involving outcomes that are clearly contrary to how matters would be if ESP—super or otherwise—were involved. These features imply the falsification of ESP as a viable explanation *of these specific cases*.

The hypothetical existence of Super-ESP has rendered itself unfalsifiable in general with the addition of *ad hoc* auxiliary hypotheses. Yet for Braude the nonfalsifiability of the Super-ESP hypothesis is not a serious issue:

One should not make too much of the non-falsifiability of psi hypotheses. Even if hypothesis H is non-falsifiable, there may still be other grounds for deciding between H and rival theses—for example, higher level pragmatic considerations concerning theoretic systematicity, explanatory fecundity, and conceptual cost. Besides, the non-falsifiability of an hypothesis may simply reflect the intractable nature of the phenomenon in question, rather than a theoretical deficiency, or the fact that the phenomenon does not exist. Widespread, large scale and inconspicuous *psi* would be the sort of phenomenon whose existence might never be conclusively demonstrated or disproved.[203]

Braude's appeal to "higher level pragmatic considerations concerning theoretic systematicity, explanatory fecundity, and conceptual cost" is, to an empiricist, just fancy-sounding nonsense. There are no "higher level" considerations: the *only* consideration for an empirical thinker is finding the inference that stands as the best explanation for all the facts at hand. An imaginary, nonfalsifiable hypothesis with no supporting evidence should never be considered a serious rival to an explanation that *does* explain the evidence in a manner consistent with other things we have reason to believe are true: for instance, that years of practice are required to achieve expert-level performance, as this has been shown true in every field of performance that researchers have examined.

Furthermore, we have seen that in its testable form, living-agent ESP as an explanation in several specific cases *has* been falsified by the evidence (such as the medium's inability to identify Miss Warner in the case involving George Pellew, and the medium's inability to identify Albert Becker in the case involving Geza Maroczy). An explanation that is proven false by one or more known facts

---

203. Braude, "Evaluating the Super-psi Hypothesis," 35.

cannot be the best explanation. And an explanation that can salvage itself only with the invention of speculative "just-so" stories is the product of fantasy, and fantasy should never be allowed to trump evidence.

And this is far from the only problem with living-agent ESP as an "explanation." The *most* a superpowerful form of living-agent ESP by itself can even possibly explain is the rapid flow of accurate information concerning the deceased provided by the medium. We must speculate—with no supporting evidence—that the medium in trance suddenly gains omniscient powers of telepathy, enabling her to telepathically gain information from the minds of others, regardless of what those others happen to be thinking about at the time, and regardless of whether or not those others are known to the medium. Also, we must speculate that the medium in trance suddenly gains omniscient powers of clairvoyance, enabling her to instantly gain access to books around the world, regardless of where those books may be located, and regardless of whether or not the medium even knows of their existence. Then, all this information from disparate sources needs to be instantly collated and presented in a coherent fashion.

But this is not enough. In order to account for the cases in which the messages indicate the purpose of the departed but not that of the medium or sitters, or are from the distinct perspective of the departed, Super-ESP requires the *ad hoc* addition of the medium's unconscious mind acting in a deceptive manner in order to pull off an elaborate hoax.

And even this is not enough. Even if we grant—for the sake of argument—that the medium possesses the staggeringly vast powers of ESP required to *instantly* telepathically or clairvoyantly acquire the facts needed in these communications, we simply have no evidence that *any* magnitude of perception, extrasensory

or otherwise, can enable an individual to brilliantly and success-
fully impersonate someone they have never met; to instantly and
temporally acquire a level of skill that required that same person
years of practice to acquire; and to reproduce the unique mental
characteristics of that person. In these cases, we are dealing not
only with a difference in the *magnitude* of an ability, but of *type*.
Braude's comment that "we simply have no decent idea what (if
any) magnitude of phenomena is implausible or unlikely, once we
have allowed psi to occur at all" is simply irrelevant.

As mentioned, "psi" refers to extrasensory perception *plus* psychokinesis (meaning the manipulation of physical objects using
only the mind). Yet including the alleged ability called psychokinesis in this discussion is also entirely irrelevant: *none* of the five
lines of evidence discussed above involved manipulating physical
objects. As mentioned earlier, the scandalous aspect of physical
mediumship persuaded the SPR to abandon all investigation into
physical mediumship, and to concentrate instead on mental mediumship. As such, *only extrasensory perception* between living persons should be offered as a possible explanation of some aspects of
the five lines of evidence. *Psi* is a vague and mysterious-seeming
term, and it is easy to be fooled into thinking that it may refer to
something more than extrasensory perception *plus* psychokinesis
(spoon bending and the like). Clarity of thought can only be promoted if we keep our terms as clear, precise, and as well defined
as possible.[204] But, to repeat the point, we simply have no reason
to believe that *any* magnitude of perception, extrasensory or otherwise, can explain the convincing impersonation and display of
high-level skills we have seen on record.

---

204. See Appendix V for a fuller discussion of this point.

To be fair, Braude does deal briefly with the sudden appearance of skills not normally apparent. But he does not deal directly with the issues above, but instead skirts tentatively around the edges. For instance, Braude writes:

> For now, let's ignore the questions arising in connection with the persistence of a deceased person's *idiosyncratic* abilities, such as a distinctively quirky sense of humor or highly specialized technical expertise. Let's focus now on more general abilities, such as the ability to write or speak in a foreign language, play a musical instrument, compose music, discuss theoretical physics, or solve mathematical problems, never mind the singular forms the abilities might take. If a non-survivalist hypothesis can't account for these general competencies, we needn't worry about more highly specialized forms.[205]

Braude elaborates:

> Consider the sorts of things that can interfere with skill development, even when we have opportunities to practice ... learning of any kind is often highly resistance-laden; it can be hampered by an endless number of interfering beliefs, insecurities, and other fears ... However, these physical, cognitive, and emotional obstacles can be overcome relatively easily in hypnotic or other profoundly altered states. For example, under the influence of stage hypnotists, good hypnotic subjects do things they've never done before—for example, dance the tango, accurately imitate their boss (or various farm animals).[206]

However, Michael Nash, editor in chief of the *International Journal of Clinical and Experimental Hypnosis*, has written: "Performance following hypnotic suggestions for learning does not

---

205. Braude, *Immortal Remains*, 114.
206. Braude, *Immortal Remains*, 116.

exceed what can be accomplished by motivated subjects outside hypnosis."[207]

Under hypnosis, subjects may lose normal inhibitions, and imitate their boss and various farm animals, but they do not speak a language they have never learned, or brilliantly impersonate people they have never met.

Braude then describes:

> A subject who, under hypnosis, started behaving and spouting New-Age platitudes like a contemporary channel or medium…[The] subject adopted novel speech patterns, tone of voice, and the awkward body language presumably appropriate to one who finds himself in strange body and unexpected surroundings. To my knowledge, this subject hadn't previously displayed the capacity to produce spontaneously consistent dramatic impersonations. And it's reasonable to think that hypnosis enabled him to accomplish what his normal fears and inhibitions might otherwise have prevented. More generally, it's plausible that manifesting a skill might be facilitated if the process bypasses the normal states in which our inhibitions and other constraints are strongest.[208]

Does Braude actually believe there is a serious comparison between portraying a crude caricature—"spouting New-Age platitudes like a contemporary channel or medium"—and the cases we have covered that involved impersonations of a *specific* deceased individual unknown to the medium, impersonations that utterly convinced those who had intimately known the living individual that they were indeed conversing with their old friend? Braude's speculation that "it's *plausible* that manifesting [that is, displaying] a skill *might* be facilitated" perhaps may somehow be drawn from

207. Nash, "The Truth and the Hype of Hypnosis," 53.
208. Braude, *Immortal Remains*, 116.

his example. But both the example and his comments on hypnosis are completely irrelevant to the mediumship and reincarnation cases covered earlier.

With regard to the impressive display of skills shown in cases of reincarnation and mediumship, Braude claims that "the *acquisition* of skills may not be the issue. All we're entitled to discuss, strictly speaking, is the *manifestation* of skills. We have no idea whether or to what extent new skills have been acquired by mediums or by subjects of reincarnation investigations. This isn't a trivial distinction, because although practice seems essential to *perfecting* a skill, it's *not* always needed to manifest skills for the first time."[209]

But it is simply not true that "we have no idea whether or to what extent new skills have been acquired by mediums or by subjects of reincarnation investigations." Is Braude asking us to seriously entertain the possibility that Bishen Chand's parents had no idea that their six-year-old son had been spending hours practicing on drums? Or that a respected judge had no idea that his daughter had taught herself to understand and fluently speak nine or ten foreign languages? Or that Mrs. Coombe-Tennant—a busy woman indeed—may have been secretly studying classical philosophy to an expert level, a subject that utterly bored both her awake and entranced self? Or that a man with an impeccable reputation for honesty secretly spent years attaining master-level expertise in chess?

With regard for the necessity of practice, Braude then writes "musical prodigies such as Mozart…usually manifest exceptional skills prior to perfecting or developing them through practice…Mozart was able to write down a complex piece of music while composing another one in his head but to my knowledge there's no evidence that he first had to practice that skill."[210]

209. Braude, *Immortal Remains*, 117.
210. Braude, *Immortal Remains*, 117–18.

The only problem with this story about Mozart is that it is simply a myth. As Colvin writes,

> Mozart's method of composing was not quite the wonder it was long thought to be … many people have believed that he had a miraculous ability to compose entire major pieces in his head. That view was based on a famous letter … the trouble is, this letter is a forgery. Mozart did not conceive whole works in his mind, perfect and complete. Surviving manuscripts show that Mozart was constantly revising, reworking, crossing out and rewriting whole sections. He wrote music the way ordinary humans do.[211]

And it is clear that Mozart certainly did attain his skills through decades of intense practice and training:

> From the earliest age, Wolfgang was receiving heavy instruction from an expert teacher who lived with him. His early compositions still seem remarkable, but it's interesting to note that the manuscripts are not in the boy's own hand. Leopold always "corrected" them before anyone saw them. It seems noteworthy also that Leopold stopped composing at just the time he began teaching Wolfgang.
>
> Mozart's first work regarded today as a masterpiece is his Piano Concerto No. 9, composed when he was twenty-one. That's certainly an early age, but we must remember that by then Wolfgang had been through eighteen years of extremely hard, expert training.[212]

Finally, the New Yorker's music critic Alex Ross has summed up the recent research on the "prodigy" Mozart: "Ambitious parents who are currently playing the 'Baby Mozart' video for their tod-

---

211. Colvin, *Talent is Overrated*, 27.
212. Colvin, *Talent is Overrated*, 25–6.

dlers may be disappointed to learn that Mozart became Mozart by working furiously hard."[213]

It should be clear that Braude's treatment of the need for practice to demonstrate impressive skill is entirely speculative and based upon serious misconceptions. And, as far as I am aware, he has continued to "ignore the questions arising in connection with the persistence of a deceased person's *idiosyncratic* abilities," precisely the sort of abilities that were clearly on display in several of the cases covered earlier.

---

213. Quoted in Colvin, 29.

Conclusion

We have covered a lot of material in this book. In Part I we considered the fundamental scientific, philosophic, and even legal issues that form the very foundations on which the case for survival is built. In Part II we carefully examined several remarkable cases supporting survival from five independent lines of evidence and used the tools from Part I to critically evaluate the skeptical objections. In this, the last chapter of the book, we are ready to sum up what we have learned, and to examine the current state of play in the survival versus Super-ESP debate. And finally, we will arrive at a sturdy conclusion.

First of all, here is a summary of the problems with the Super-ESP hypothesis:

- Provides no positive evidence, merely proposes imaginary possibilities.
- Attempts to shift the burden of proof away from those offering Super-ESP as a counterexplanation, and toward the defenders of survival to prove that these imaginary possibilities are *not* true.

- Ignores the distinction between proof beyond all reasonable doubt, and proof beyond all conceivable doubt.
- Mistakenly argues that objecting to Super-ESP as an explanation of any particular case is to make an assumption about the limits to the possible magnitude of extrasensory perception.
- Living-agent ESP has rendered itself unfalsifiable with the addition of *ad hoc* auxiliary assumptions, such as the cunningly deceptive behavior of the medium's unconscious mind, and by extending the nature of extrasensory perception to include abilities that have nothing to do with *any* form of perception, extrasensory or otherwise, and so has become the ideology of *Super*-ESP.

The fact that the fundamental issues discussed in Part I of this book have not been made explicit by proponents of Super-ESP has set a trap into which even otherwise sophisticated thinkers have fallen. After summarizing the survival versus Super-ESP debate, one such thinker recently wrote:

This brief and abstract description will serve, I hope, to illustrate the general flavor of these debates, which seem to many well-informed observers to have arrived at **a logical impasse**. The core problem hinges on the fact that **information** provided by an ostensibly surviving communicator can only be verified by reference to information which is known to some living person or persons, or objectively documented in some other fashion, and hence which is also in principle potentially accessible to some sort of psi process. It is therefore always **possible to invent scenarios** according to which apparent evidence of survival can be "explained" alternatively in terms of psi processes involving only living persons. Such scenarios may need to be fantastically complex, but psi has been shown in various experimental contexts to operate in a "goal-oriented" manner unaffected by the apparent "complexity" of its tasks, and consequently they cannot be decisively refuted. But note the real **logical peculiarity** here: It is not that we have positive knowledge that psi processes *can* accomplish the extraordinary things required by such explanations, but rather that we are presently unable to prove that they *cannot*.[214]

The first and most obvious problem with this is that it refers only to the *information* provided by mediums. But as we have clearly seen, in the best cases much more than mere information is provided. In the best cases we have also seen evidence of the purpose, perspective, personality, acquired skills, and modes of active thinking distinctive of the departed person in question. And no magnitude of psi—extrasensory perception plus psychokinesis—is capable of accounting for the demonstration of the latter three.

A second problem with this is that although there may be "a logical impasse," there is no impasse in terms of evidence. For all the reasons listed in chapter 3, in both law and science, the burden of proof, of providing evidence, is on the person making the claim. For instance, before a criminal case can go to trial, the prosecution must appear before a grand jury to make an evidence-based *prima facie* case that the accused did indeed commit the crime in question. If during trial the defense attorney argues, "Well, it's *possible* that the investigating detectives acted in a conspiracy to frame my client," and offers no supporting evidence, then any competent prosecuting attorney will object on grounds that the theory is pure speculation, and any competent judge will sustain the objection. It is not required in a court of law that the prosecution prove that the police did *not* frame the accused. And, at the risk of seeming repetitive, this

---

214. Kelly et al., *Irreducible Mind*, 597. Bold emphasis added.

is because the burden of proof on the prosecution is proof beyond all reasonable doubt, not proof beyond all conceivable doubt, and allowing purely imaginary possibilities into the argument raises the burden of proof from the former to the latter, an impossible standard to meet when dealing with empirical matters.

A mere logical possibility is not a real possibility unless there are evidence-based reasons to believe it may actually be true. We may agree with the author that "it is always possible to invent scenarios" to support an explanation in terms of ESP, but "inventing scenarios" is not the same as providing evidence. And evidence-based arguments are the only arguments appropriate in empirical matters, such as those dealt with in law, science, and history. Many academic philosophers—most of whom gain no experience in their careers of evaluating evidence—tend to forget this, and assume that purely speculative arguments of the type offered by the proponents of Super-ESP have some validity in empirical matters. They do not. The proponents of survival have put forward a strong *prima facie* case; it is not required of them that they prove that imagined psi processes *cannot* accomplish the extraordinary things required by such "explanations." The burden of proof should properly be placed on the proponents of Super-ESP to provide evidence that psi processes involving only the living *can be and were* employed in specific cases to simulate an unconscious deception that a deceased personality has communicated.

Finally, the author asks us to "note the real logical peculiarity here: It is not that we have positive knowledge that psi processes *can* accomplish the extraordinary things required by such explanations, but rather that we are presently unable to prove that they *cannot*."[215]

---

215. Once again, note that the possible existence of Super-ESP has the same logical status as the imaginary possibility that we live in the Matrix. Can you prove that we do not?

And here we see the third problem: not only is the burden of providing evidence shifted away from the proponents of Super-ESP; in addition, any theory that *cannot* be proven false is untestable. It is therefore not a scientific theory, and so must be classified as metaphysics at best, ideology at worst.

The reader will recall that the existence of Super-ESP was first proposed when the proxy sittings made it clear that ordinary extrasensory perception between mediums and sitters could not explain the evidence. Although the theory was falsified, it was not abandoned: it was simply stretched and extended to fantastic lengths until it could no longer be refuted. It should thus be clear that the motivation behind the idea of Super-ESP is ideological, not scientific: it was proposed for the sole purpose of opposing an explanation that simply and elegantly accounts for all the best evidence for survival.

Nobel Laureate physicist Robert Laughlin has written:

> A key symptom of ideological thinking is the explanation that has no implications and cannot be tested. I call such logical dead-ends anti-theories because they have exactly the opposite effect of real theories: they stop thinking rather than stimulate it.[216]

It is time we stopped giving the Super-ESP anti-theory the respect it does not deserve.

• • •

Using the technique of inference to the best explanation, an inference may be reached in a purely deductive manner.

Here is the argument in point form:

---

216. Quoted in Lennox, *God's Undertaker?*, 158.

1. We have seen that the best evidence from mediumship not only includes a rapid display of highly complex information, but also involves clear indications of the personalities, acquired skills, and unique mental characteristics distinctive of the minds of certain individuals who once lived on Earth.

2. We do not have the slightest reason to believe that the use of mere *perception*—extrasensory or otherwise—can enable anyone to reproduce these three features.

3. The only source we know of that can instantly produce these features are the minds of individuals known to possess these personalities, acquired skills, and unique mental characteristics.

4. It is rational to prefer an argument that explains the evidence in terms consistent with what we know to be true over one that does not.

5. Hence, the rational inference must be that the best explanation for this evidence is the survival and continuing exercise of the capacities of said minds.

And, we have seen that survival also provides the best explanation of the data for near-death experiences, deathbed visions, apparitions, and memories of previous lives, in addition to the data from mediumship. Five independent lines of evidence, all very different from each other, all pointing in the same direction, and all explained by one simple and elegant explanation: the continuing survival of the minds of the departed, with their distinctive purposes, perspectives, personalities, skills, and unique mental characteristics both intact and clearly evident.

Epilogue

It is naïve to assume that the arguments and evidence presented here will result in all the materialists and believers in Super-ESP simply changing their opinion, just as it is naïve to think that arguments and evidence are capable of changing the opinions of all of those who believe, without a shred of supporting evidence, that the moon landings were faked in a film studio; that the United States presidential election of 2020 was stolen through massive voter fraud; and that the data for man-made global heating is the result of a conspiracy involving climate scientists around the world.

However, if you choose to delve further into the literature on survival, you will find that there is no shortage of scientists and scholars who started off as die-hard skeptics, and yet after spending years of long and rigorous hands-on study of mediums for the sole purpose of debunking them, not only changed their minds, but also had the courage to openly admit that they had been wrong. These men and women deserve our admiration and our gratitude.

A few personal points may be in order:

If I had never carefully studied the various works of the "skeptics" of survival, I would still be wondering if I were indeed a living example of Feynman's famous dictum. In that sense, I owe them a debt. For by now, the true nature of their desperately contrived objections should be obvious to you.

And finally, I would like to thank my old college friend Barry, who, all those years ago, convinced me to spend a year living in a haunted farmhouse.

Appendix I
Quantum Mechanics

> If a person does not feel shocked when he
> first encounters quantum theory, he has not
> understood a word of it.
> —Niels Bohr

Up until the moment of measurement certain properties of quantum phenomena—such as location, momentum, direction of spin—simply exist as a collection of probabilities, known as the wave function. The wave function can be thought of as the probability distribution of all possible states, such as, for instance, the probability distribution of all possible locations for an electron.[217] But this is not the probability that the electron is actually *at* certain locations: it is the probability that the electron *will be found* at certain locations. The electron *does not have a definite location* until it is observed. Upon measurement this collection of all possible locations "collapses" to a single value: the location of the particle that is actually observed.

---

217. More technically, the probability distribution is the absolute square of the wave function.

Physicist Nick Herbert expresses it this way:

> The quantum physicist treats the atom as a wave of oscillating possibilities as long as it is not observed. But whenever it is looked at, the atom stops vibrating and objectifies one of its many possibilities. Whenever someone chooses to look at it, the atom ceases its fuzzy dance and seems to "freeze" into a tiny object with definite attributes, only to dissolve once more into a quivering pool of possibilities as soon as the observer withdraws his attention from it. The apparent observer-induced change in an atom's mode of existence is called the *collapse of the wave function.*[218]

Measurements thus play a more positive role in quantum mechanics than in classical physics, because here they are not merely observations of something already present, but actually help produce it. According to one interpretation of quantum mechanics popular among many theorists, it is the existence of consciousness that introduces intrinsic probability into the quantum world.

As mentioned, objects do not have definite properties for certain attributes, such as position, velocity, or direction of spin, until they are measured. It is not simply that these properties are unknown until they are observed: they do not *exist* in any definite state until they are measured.

Prior to observation the particle exists in a state Schrödinger termed *superposition*: the electron, atom (or any other particle) exists with its dynamic properties—that is, those that can take a range of values—in an indefinite state, simultaneously existing with a range of possible values, none of which are definite until

---

218. Herbert, *Elemental Mind*, 145–146.

observed.[219] It is thought that this state of superposition gives rise to the wavelike nature of the particle's behavior.

Before detection, an electron is not actually a physical wave (in the sense that a light wave or water wave is a wave), but rather, because the equation governing its behavior is wavelike, the actual detection of its dynamic properties upon observation demonstrates wavelike behavior.

The wave function is a *wave of probability,* a mathematical description of the state of a particle at various points in time; it is used to predict the *probable* values of various particle properties that will be observed upon observation, such as position and velocity. The square of the wave function is used to derive the probabilities of the various possible values of these variables upon observation, when the wave function collapses and only a single value is observed. Note that the wave function changes and evolves over time: it is dynamic, not static.

This conclusion is based, in part, on the famous "two-slit" experiment, in which electrons are fired one at a time at a barrier with two slits. Measuring devices on a screen behind the barrier indicate that the electrons seem to behave as waves, going through both slits simultaneously, with patterns of interference typical of wave phenomena: wave crests arriving simultaneously at the same place in time will reinforce each other; waves and troughs arriving simultaneously at the same place will cancel each other (interference patterns result when two wave fronts meet, for instance, after dropping two stones into a pond). These waves are only thought of as *probability* waves—or "wave functions"—as they do not carry any energy, and so cannot be directly detected. Only individual electrons

---

219. Dynamic properties—such as position or velocity—may take a range of possible values, as compared to static properties, such as mass or charge, which always have the same fixed value.

are detected by the measuring device on the screen behind the barrier, but the *distribution* of numerous electrons shows the interference patterns typical of waves. It is as though each unobserved electron exists in a wavelike form until it arrives at the screen to be detected, at which time its actual location (the place the particle is actually observed on the screen) can only be predicted statistically— according to the interference pattern of its wave function.

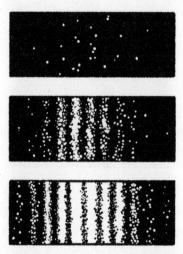

Stages of the two-slit interference pattern.
As more electrons hit the screen, an interference
pattern gradually emerges.

If, however, a measuring device is placed at the slits, then each electron is observed to pass through only one slit, and no interference pattern in the distribution of electrons is observed. The explanation is that the wave function now collapses at the slits, instead of at the screen. In other words, electrons behave as waves when not observed, but as particles in a definite location when observed! All quantum entities—electrons, protons, photons, and so on—display this wave-particle duality, behaving as wave or particle, depending on whether or not they are directly observed.

With detectors at the slits, no interference pattern
emerges on the screen as electrons are detected.

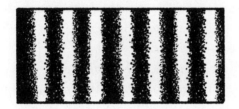

Wavelike interference pattern that emerges
with no detectors at the slits.

The double-slit experiment is one example of Rosenblum and Kuttner's point made earlier in the discussion of dualism:

No energy need be involved in determining to *which particular* situation a wavefunction collapses. Thus, the determination of which of the physically possible conscious experiences becomes the actual experience is a process that need not involve energy transfer. Quantum mechanics therefore allow an escape from the supposed fatal flaw of dualism. It is a mistake to think that dualism can be ruled out on the basis of physics.

Note that although the double-slit experiment is one example of this point, the argument really applies to any quantum system *in which we have a choice of how we observe the situation.* Modern physics—it is argued by many—brings mind back into nature, as it plays a fundamental role in the collapse of the wave function (see chapter 4 of my book *Science and the Near-Death Experience* for a fuller explanation of the role of mind in physics, including the reason why measuring instruments cannot by themselves collapse the wave function: in a nutshell, being physical, there is no reason to think that measuring instruments are exempt from the quantum rules, and so must also exist in a state of superposition until observed). This point also illustrates Henry Stapp's comment that "contemporary physical theory allows, and its orthodox von Neumann form entails, an interactive dualism that is fully in accord with all the laws of physics."

Quantum physics replaces the deterministic clockwork picture of the universe portrayed by classical physics: at its most fundamental level, the behavior of the universe is essentially random.

Albert Einstein, one of the architects of quantum mechanics, never liked the randomness of quantum theory. He believed that quantum mechanics was incomplete, and that when some other, more fundamental theory was developed, the seeming randomness would vanish. For decades Einstein and his friend Niels Bohr frequently debated the meaning and interpretation of quantum physics.[220]

Finally, we should note that quantum mechanical uncertainty may have an interesting theological implication, as the following quotes reveal.

> God does not play dice with the cosmos.
> —Albert Einstein

---

220. It is generally agreed that Bohr eventually won all these debates. An excellent book to read on the history of quantum mechanics is *Quantum: Einstein, Bohr, and the Great Debate about the Nature of Reality,* by Manjit Kumar.

Einstein, stop telling God what to do!
—Niels Bohr

If you want to build a robust universe, one that will never go wrong, then you don't want to build it like a clock, for the smallest bit of grit could cause it to go awry. However, if things at base are utterly random, nothing can make them more disordered. Complete randomness at the heart of things is the most stable situation imaginable—a divinely clever way to build a sturdy universe.
—Heinz Pagels

Appendix II

Near-Death Experiences of the Blind

Dozens of cases of NDEs occurring to blind people have been carefully studied, and the majority report an experience of sight—including those who were blind since birth.

For decades there had been rumors of NDEs occurring to blind people, in which they could clearly see their surroundings while seemingly outside of their bodies. But these stories remained little more than unsubstantiated anecdotes until researchers Kenneth Ring and Sharon Cooper launched an in-depth investigation of NDEs in the blind and published their results in a book they titled *Mindsight*.

These researchers found twenty-one cases in which blind people had an NDE, which was defined as "any type of conscious experience associated with a condition that was unquestionably life-threatening, regardless of whether it conformed to the familiar classic pattern of the Moody-type NDE."[221] Out of these twenty-one cases, fifteen blind individuals claimed to have some sort of sight during their NDE, three were not sure whether they saw or not, and the remain-

---

221. Ring and Cooper, *Mindsight*, 16.

ing three did not appear to see at all. Ring and Cooper also collected ten cases of OBEs not associated with a medical crisis, and here the figures are even more impressive: nine out of ten blind people claimed to have had sight while they remembered being out of their bodies (the other person was not sure). Their total sample included fourteen individuals blind from birth, and from among this group nine individuals, or 64 percent, reported sight during an NDE or OBE.

Ring and Cooper summarize what the blind tend to report seeing in these circumstances.

> In general, blind people report the same kinds of visual impressions as sighted persons do in describing NDEs and OBEs. For example, ten of our twenty-one NDErs said they had some kind of vision of their physical body, and seven of our ten OBErs said likewise. Occasionally, there are other this-worldly perceptions as well, such as seeing a medical team at work on one's body or seeing various features of the room or surroundings where one's physical body was. Otherworldly perceptions abound also, and seem to take the form characteristic for transcendental NDEs of sighted persons—radiant light, otherworldly landscapes, angels or religious figures, deceased relatives, and so forth.[222]

These visual perceptions also tended to be "extremely clear and detailed, especially when they found themselves in the otherworldly portions of their near-death journeys."[223]

Cardiologist Peter Fenwick reported the following case involving an American woman he refers to as Emily. Born premature, Emily was blinded by excess oxygen in her incubator at the age

---

222. Ring and Cooper, *Mindsight*, 75.
223. Ring and Cooper, *Mindsight*, 76.

of three months. When she was twenty-two Emily was in a road accident and spent three days in a coma.

> The first thing I clearly remember was being on the ceiling, looking down, and seeing this body. I was really terrified by the ability to see. At first, I couldn't relate to that body, and then I realized it was me. I could hear the doctor telling the others: "There's blood on her eardrum. Now she's probably going to be deaf as well as blind." I was screaming at him, "But I can hear! I can hear!" and I felt this terrible desolation because I couldn't get through to him. Then the nurse said that I'd be in a vegetative state. I tried to talk to her, but she couldn't hear me either.
>
> Then I was pulled up through the roof and I had this glorious sense of freedom. I could move wherever I wanted to. I was above the street, above the hospital, and I was ecstatic about being able to move wherever I wanted to. Then that ended suddenly. I was sucked into a tunnel, and heard a sound like monstrous fans. It was not actually that, but it's the closest way I can describe it. It was a beautiful sound. The tunnel was dark, with regular open spaces in the side, through which I could see other people travelling in other tunnels. There was one area I passed by where there was a group of drab, dull, unhappy people who were unable to move. Then I saw the distant light, and I heard these hymns. The light got brighter, and I saw Him. I saw Christ. He was incredibly beautiful. His feet were bare. He was wearing a bright garment. The bosom was open and you could see his chest. He had hair down to his shoulders and a beard. There was light in and around his head, and coming out of his head like a star.[224]

The Fenwicks describe how "five people came to meet Emily: two close school friends who had died, an old couple who had once been neighbors, and her grandmother. Jesus forbade her to

---

224. Fenwick and Fenwick, *The Truth in the Light*, 86.

touch any of them, telling her it was not her time yet, she had to go back and live and have children."

This was followed by a very detailed life review, in which she was able to feel not only how she felt at the time, but also the feelings of everyone else involved. Then she felt a jolt, heard the sound of rushing wind, and suddenly found herself back in her body.

Those who wish to debunk this and similar cases may question *how* a person blind virtually since birth could conjure up visual images. However, at this point we would do well to recall the discussion above in "the extraordinary claims" section regarding the logical distinction between knowing *that* something occurred and being able to explain *how* it occurred.

And so, with the wisdom and humility of a true scientist, Dr. Fenwick concluded his account with a serious consideration of "the alternative that somehow in the NDE she truly did see. Science at present has no explanation for this ... [However] perhaps we should not dismiss Emily's claim to have 'seen' in her NDE, even though we do not know what mechanism might have been involved."[225]

225. Fenwick and Fenwick, *The Truth in the Light*, 87.

Appendix III
Why Does What We Believe Matter?

Philosopher David Griffen recently issued this dire warning:

> I believe the human race now faces the greatest challenge in its history. If it continues on its present course, widespread misery and death of unprecedented proportions is a certainty. Annihilation of human life and of millions of species of non-human life as well is probable. This is so because of polluting technologies, economic growth-mania, out-of-control population growth, global apartheid between rich and poor nations, rapid depletion of non-renewable resources, and proliferation of nuclear weapons combined with a state of international anarchy that makes war inevitable and sufficient measures to halt global ecological destruction impossible.
>
> What seems clear is that a transition in world *order*, if it is to occur, will have to be accompanied by a shift in world *view*, one that would lead to a new sense of adventure, replacing the modern adventure of unending economic growth based on the technological subjugation of nature. Only if we come to see human life as primarily a spiritual adventure, an adventurous journey that continues beyond this life, will we have a chance of becoming

sufficiently free from destructive motivations to affect a transition to a sustainable global order.[226]

Griffen offers several practical benefits of a belief in an afterlife:

1. Such a belief can help overcome the fear of death and extermination.
2. If people are convinced that they are ultimately not subject to any earthly power, this can increase their courage to fight for freedom, ecologically sustainable policies, and social justice.
3. If people believe that this life is not the final word, and that justice will prevail in the next life, this can help them withstand the unfairness they encounter in the here-and-now.
4. The idea of life as an unfolding journey, which continues even after death, can lead to a greater sense of connection with the universe as it unfolds into the future.
5. The belief in life after death can help counter the extreme degree of materialism that has pervaded every niche of modern civilization.
6. The belief that we are on a spiritual journey, and that we have time to reach our destination, can motivate us to think creatively about what we can do now—socially, internationally, and individually—to move closer to what we should be in the here-and-now.

---

226. Griffen, *Parapsychology, Philosophy, and Spirituality*, 291–292.

Appendix IV

Is ESP a "Simpler" Explanation Than Survival?

As we have seen, the ESP objection to mediumship as evidence of survival combines the extrasensory capabilities of the medium with the dramatizing powers of her subconscious mind. It is alleged that the medium picks up information telepathically or clairvoyantly, and then "dresses it up" in the form of an imitation of a personality. It is asserted that this is a more economical explanation of the communications: we already have independent evidence that telepathy and clairvoyance exist, and so—it is argued—an explanation in terms of ESP is "simpler" than the hypothesis that further assumes discarnate survival.

The philosopher Curt Ducasse carefully considered this and made a very insightful comment:

> It [has been] urged that possession of such powers by the medium is a more economical explanation of the contents and style of the communications; for the medium is anyway known to exist and so is extrasensory perception; whereas the spirit survival explanation requires one to assume gratuitously (1) that spirits exist; (2) that they are capable of remembering; (3) that they are capable of

temporarily "possessing" the body of some living persons; and (4) that they are capable of telepathic communication with some living persons.

The first comment these criticisms invite is that, in discussions of the question of survival, clarity of thought is promoted if, for one thing, one leaves out altogether the weasel word "spirits," and uses instead the word "minds"; the question then being whether there is any evidence that minds that were incarnate continue to exist and to function discarnate, thus surviving their body's death.

When the question of survival is formulated thus in terms not of "spirits" but of *minds*, then the allegation that the survival explanation makes gratuitously the four assumptions mentioned above is seen to be erroneous. For (1) that there are minds is not an assumption but a known fact; (2) that minds are capable of remembering is likewise not an assumption but is known; (3) that minds are capable of "possessing" living human bodies is also a known fact, for "possession" is but the name of the *normal* relation of a mind to its living body. *Paranormal* "possession" would be a possession in the very same sense, but only temporary, and of a living body by a mind other than its own—that other mind being one which had been that of a body now dead; and (4) that telepathic communication between minds is possible and also a known fact.[227]

Why Is Simplicity Desirable?

Complexity itself cannot be the issue: both relativity and quantum mechanics are more complex, both conceptually and mathematically, than the simpler Newtonian mechanics. And yet the reason they superseded Newtonian mechanics is that they can account for everything the classical theory accounts for, and also for phe-

---

227. Ducasse, "What Would Constitute Conclusive Evidence of Survival after Death?" 402–3.

nomena that are completely inexplicable by the simpler classical theory. As Oxford philosopher of science John Lennox summed up, "The reason that such complex physical theories are accepted by scientists is not because of their simplicity; it is because of their [greater] explanatory power."[228]

What is not permitted by a rational philosophy of science is *unnecessary* complexity. This is what is meant by William of Occam's famous dictum "do not multiply entities beyond what is necessary." If momentum and gravity are sufficient to explain the orbits of the planets, then do not add the efforts of invisible angels. Of greater importance, if your theory of orbital motion is refuted by the evidence, then do not add the efforts of invisible angels to render your theory immune from being proven false by any form of evidence.

For instance, the Newtonian theory of orbital motion predicted the orbits of planets with astonishing accuracy; it did not predict the orbit of Mercury with complete accuracy, but this did not trouble many. But in the early twentieth century the rival theory of general relativity emerged, and it more accurately accounted for the orbit of Mercury than the simpler classical theory. If at this point the defenders of classical mechanics had added untestable auxiliary assumptions—such as the work of invisible angels—in order to render the theory unfalsifiable, then they would have turned a testable scientific theory into dogma, unworthy of further serious consideration.

But this is precisely what is required of the defenders of living-agent ESP. Note the contrived nature of the theory: whenever we provide reasons why the medium's powers of extrasensory perception cannot explain the evidence for survival in any particular

---

228. Lennox, *God's Undertaker?*, 180.

case, the defenders are then forced to invent *ad hoc* speculations of remarkable *unconscious* motivations and abilities in order to explain away the objectionable case, thereby rendering the living-agent ESP theory immune from falsification. We have seen several examples of this, perhaps most clearly in the apparition and mediumship cases.

These *ad hoc* auxiliary speculated abilities are the "invisible angels" of Super-ESP, which give no new predictions in exchange for increased complexity. In other words, the defenders have no recourse but to turn the living-agent theory into dogma, ideology, an anti-theory whose sole purpose is to oppose an explanation that simply and elegantly accounts for all the best evidence for survival.

The contrived and *ad hoc* nature of Super-ESP explanations should by now be obvious. We have examined five independent lines of evidence for survival, all very different from each other, and all accounted for by one simple and elegant explanation: the survival of the minds of the departed, period. By contrast, not only does Super-ESP require a different form of extrasensory perception to explain each of the five independent lines of evidence, it also requires a different *just-so* story to explain *each case* within each of the five lines of evidence.

Appendix V
Super-ESP or "Living-Agent Psi"?

Psi (the second to last letter of the Greek alphabet, pronounced *sigh*) is a catchall term that refers to extrasensory perception plus psychokinesis (the supposed ability to influence the motion of objects using only the mind). We have seen above that some skeptics of survival speculate that psi operating only between living-agents can somehow explain the evidence for survival.

But it should be clear that psychokinesis is simply irrelevant in any discussion of the best evidence: soon after their founding in the 1880s, the British and American Societies for Psychical Research abandoned all investigation of physical mediumship for good reasons, and so the term *psi* is simply redundant.

"Psi" sounds mysterious, and it is easy to imagine that the term refers to something more than merely extrasensory perception plus the hypothetical ability to mentally influence the motion of objects (such as bending spoons *à la* Uri Geller). The more precise and relevant term is simply extrasensory perception (ESP), as the only counterexplanation for the evidence discussed in this book involves nothing more than the hypothesis of virtually unlimited powers of extrasensory *perception* among only the living (combined with the untestable conjectures of the various mediums having unconscious motives and employing unconscious deception). When we substitute "extrasensory perception plus psychokinesis" instead of the vague term *psi*, then it becomes glaringly obvious that any explanation involving nothing more than *perception plus the hypothetical ability to mentally influence the motion of objects* simply cannot bear the burden of proof required of it to explain the cases described above. We should not allow our opponents in a debate to define the key terms in a manner favorable to their own purposes, such as "health issues" instead of lung cancer, "global warming" instead of global heating, "enhanced interrogation" instead of torture, and so on.

So, should we use the term living-agent ESP or *Super*-ESP? At the use of the second term some proponents of the first term bristle, and remark that *"all* ESP is super." But this is a contradiction in terms, as the adjective *super* refers to that which is *above and beyond* the ordinary.

Consider the Ganzfeld telepathy experiments, which involve concentration and relaxation before each session, during which the receiver, in a state of sensory deprivation, relaxes his or her mind and attempts to passively receive an image that the sender is concentrating upon, in another room, carefully isolated from the receiver. After thirty minutes, the receiver is shown four pictures and asked to guess which of the four the sender was viewing. The success rate is typically around 33 percent, when 25 percent would be expected purely by chance. Nothing in the Ganzfeld results *even remotely* suggests that detailed messages can be sent. Contrast this with the Kakie case, in which seemingly normal communication—even singing—occurred between the child communicator and her living relatives. As we saw earlier, in his review of this case, researcher Dr. Alan Gauld concluded, "I know of no instance of undeniable telepathy between living persons, or for that matter of any variety of ESP, in which the flow of paranormally acquired information has been so quick, so copious, and so free from error."[229] And this case is by no means unique: several of the other mediumship cases examined also involve detailed two-way communication, and, like this one, often in real time.

The common retort is that ESP in "real-life" is more impressive. This is true, and earlier we have seen dramatic real-life examples of ESP, occurring in life-threatening situations. But ESP in the wild is almost always goal-oriented, and involves a *feeling*, such as a feeling of danger, or a feeling of being stared at. Even the most impressive of these experiences do not involve detailed and highly accurate perceptions and messages, of the sort that have been described in this book again and again.

Make no mistake: the level of extrasensory perception hypothesized to explain away the best cases borders on the omniscient. The advocate of living-agent ESP must claim that the unconscious mind of the medium has the ability to *instantly* acquire any required information telepathically from the minds of the living, regardless of what those persons are thinking about at the time, and regardless of whether or not they are known to the medium. The advocate must also claim that the medium has the ability to *instantly* acquire any required information clairvoyantly from written material in scattered locations, regardless of whether those locations are known by the medium, and regardless of whether those materials are even known by the medium to exist. Then, all this information from various sources, mental and physical, must be *instantly* and unconsciously collated into an integrated whole.

---

229. Gauld, *Mediumship and Survival*, 41.

Finally, the information must be coherently presented in the same manner as the deceased would have presented it, and packaged with the false claim that the source is the living mind of the deceased.

Thus, the advocate of living-agent ESP is forced not only to claim that the unconscious mind of the medium possesses virtually unlimited powers of extrasensory perception: the advocate must also claim that the unconscious mind of the medium is a brilliant con artist and a shameless liar toward everyone involved, including toward the conscious mind of the medium themself.

But the stark truth is that all indications, from both laboratory experiments and anecdotal reports, are that psi, at least among the living, is an extremely low-level set of abilities that cannot be used to transmit messages, or to beat the casinos. Anecdotal—that is, personal—reports of ESP are almost always limited to a sense of being stared at, or a sense of imminent danger.

The staggeringly vast magnitude of extrasensory perception required just to acquire *the facts* needed in the best cases far exceeds in power and scope anything seen in clear-cut demonstrations of ESP, inside or outside of laboratories. Let us therefore be clear: a degree of extrasensory perception among the living capable of gathering all the facts needed in the best cases most certainly fits the adjective *super*, that is, far above and beyond the ordinary.

Let us also be clear that much more than the mere acquisition of facts is required to convincingly impersonate another person who is completely or almost completely unknown to the medium: an entirely different *type* of skill is required, a skill that cannot be reduced to the mere acquisition of facts about a person, regardless of how those facts may have been acquired. And far more than the mere acquisition of facts is required to instantly and temporarily acquire the expert-level skills of the departed person who claims to be communicating, skills that required the departed person years of practice to acquire. The possible *magnitude* of extrasensory perception involved in these cases is simply irrelevant, as much more than mere *perception*, extrasensory or otherwise, is required.

Super-ESP indeed.

Appendix VI

What the Dead Say

The last chapter of my third book is devoted to various descriptions of the afterworld as relayed from several independent sources, and it is evident that the central cores of the various messages are very much in agreement. Critics may accuse writers such as myself of cherry-picking the data, but this accusation invariably comes from those whose familiarity with the literature is either little or none. It is not my intent in this brief appendix to exhaustively compare and contrast various descriptions of the afterworld, since this has been done by several writers in various books.

To mention only one example, geologist Dr. Robert Crookall resigned from his work in 1952 to devote his life to psychical research. For the next nine years he collected communications though mediums from every country he could, including Australia, Brazil, England, India, South Africa, Tibet, and the Hawaiian Islands. In 1961 he wrote *The Supreme Adventure: Analysis of Psychic Communications*, in which he described the findings of his nearly decade-long research. He had found that descriptions of the afterlife from different mediums in different parts of the world are highly similar, and closely resembled descriptions communicated via mediums in the West.

The intent here is only to provide a brief overview of what we may expect. Those readers who are interested in more detailed descriptions may track down books listed in the bibliography,[230] and may consult the final chapter of my third book.

There are of course differences in incidental details, and, as may be expected, the descriptions from those whose departures have only recently preceded the messages tend to be far more basic and limited.

Frederic Myers, the originator of the cross correspondences, had been dead twenty-three years before he began to convey descriptions of the afterworld, and from Myers come the most complete and detailed descriptions ever conveyed. As a former member of the SPR, his first concern had been to rigorously establish his identity. Once this had been accomplished, he was ready to report on his experiences and on the knowledge he had gained. These communications were recorded in two postmortem books, both dictated through the amateur trance-medium Geraldine Cummins. In these works, Myers described a stupendous journey of the immortal soul through the various planes or spheres of existence, beginning with Earth.

In his first postmortem book, Myers described the various planes of existence:

- The plane of matter
- Hades, the intermediate state
- The third plane, the sphere of terrene imagination
- Eidos
- The Plane of Flame

---

230. See for instance, Allen, 2015; Barker, 1995; Cummins, 1932 and 1935; Cummins and Toksvig, 1965; Hamilton, 1969; Sherwood, 1969.

- The Plane of Light
- Out-Yonder, flight from the physical universe

Myers described Hades, the astral plane, as nothing sinister, but merely a temporary resting place on the borders of two worlds. The time spent in Hades is said to vary with the needs of the individual, with children often requiring hardly any rest at all. However, for Myers: "I died in Italy, a land I loved, and I was very weary at the time of my passing. For me Hades was a place of rest, a place of half-lights and drowsy peace."[231]

The third plane is given various names by Myers, such as the Lotus Flower Paradise, Summerland, or the Sphere of Terrene Imagination. It is described as being very similar to Earth, but with a beauty that far transcends the terrestrial, the heaven for which humans have always yearned, and of which their various theologies had told them. Myers tells us that communities of like-minded individuals with similar tastes come together and live in mutually constructed environments, while those of a more solitary nature may live in an environment entirely devised from their own preferences and desires.

Silver Birch, communicating with the persona of the Native American he seems to have been in a terrestrial life, described the third plane with these words:

> There is nothing in your world of matter with which you can compare the life of the spirit, freed from the trammels of the flesh, escaped from the prison of the body of matter, with liberty to go where you will, to see your thoughts take shape, to follow out the desires of your heart, to be freed from the troubles of money. No, you have not tasted the joys of the world of spirit.[232]

---

231. Cummins, *The Road to Immortality*, 38.
232. Austen, *Teachings of Silver Birch*, 116, as quoted in Allen, *The Realities of Heaven*, 77.

Myers himself claimed to have ascended to the fourth plane, Eidos, according to Myers, the first true heaven-world. He described the earth as only a poor copy of the fourth plane, in his words, "A copy of a masterpiece."

> We dwell in a world of appearances in some respects similar to the earth. Only all this vast region of appearances is gigantic in conception, terrifying and exquisite according to the manner in which it presents itself to the Soul-man. It is far more fluidic, less apparently solid than earth surroundings.[233]

In this world the mind is now endowed with divine creative powers, and it uses substances and colors unknown on Earth to create an infinite variety of forms of unsurpassable beauty. The purpose of existence on this plane is to experience all the possibilities of form, so that the evolving soul may eventually pass beyond all involvement with it.

> On this luminiferous plane the struggle increases in intensity, the efforts expended are beyond the measure of earthly experience. But the results of such labour, of such intellectualized and spiritualized toil and battle also transcend the most superb emotion in the life of man. In brief, all experience is refined, heightened, intensified, and the actual zest of living is increased immeasurably.[234]

The fifth, sixth, and seventh planes are said to be increasingly difficult to describe, as they are progressively more and more remote from our earthly experience. Nevertheless, they are said to be increasingly desirable. Myers does not spend much time dis-

---

233. Cummins, *The Road to Immortality*, 57.
234. Cummins, *The Road to Immortality*, 58.

cussing these planes, but he does insist that there is no loss of individuality at any point.

Beyond the fourth plane lies the Plane of Flame, in which the individual "is as an artist who lives in his masterpiece, derives from it, in all its features, in the freshness of its evolving, changing creation, that strange exaltation which may, perhaps, at one rare moment, be known to a creative genius—though very faintly—while he still lives upon the earth."[235]

On the sixth plane,

> They are lords of life, for they have conquered. They are capable of living now without form, of existing as white light, as the pure thought of their Creator. They have joined the immortals.[236]

And when the individual has exhausted the possibilities of the sixth plane,

> The spirit which contains this strange individualized life passes out Yonder and enters into the Mystery, thereby fulfilling the final purpose, the evolution of the Supreme Mind.[237]

Myers struggled to convey what others more advanced than he had told him of the seventh state.

> The Beyond baffles description. It is heart-breaking even to attempt to write of it ... the passage from the Sixth to the Seventh state means the flight from the material universe ... You still exist as an individual. You are as a wave in the sea; and you have at last entered into Reality and cast from you all the illusions of appearances. You dwell not only outside of time but outside of the universe on this last plane of being.[238]

235. Cummins, *The Road to Immortality*, 69.
236. Cummins, *The Road to Immortality*, 71.
237. Cummins, *The Road to Immortality*, 71.
238. Cummins, *The Road to Immortality*, 72–3.

Many Mansions

Many communicators, including Myers, describe how there are both different regions and subdivisions within each of the planes. The regions of these planes in which we spend most of our time depends upon our interests, desires, and temperaments. Communicators often insist that the region we first encounter within the third plane also depends on how we lived our earthly lives, and upon our level of moral and spiritual development. Not everyone enjoys an idyllic existence on the third plane: the lower levels are described as dark, gloomy, desolate, in which there are no children, but only those who, as adults on Earth, had chosen to lead selfish, evil lives. How long they remain in this nether region depends on how long they choose to remain in a selfish, morally undeveloped state. Assistance and teaching are offered by benevolent visitors from worlds above, but it seems that many denizens of these quasi-hellish domains scorn these efforts; at least at first.

The Fate of the Cruel Person

According to Myers, the cruel man does not find paradise on the third plane. Instead, he languishes in a state of mental distress, until,

> Eventually, this individual faces up to his own misery, to his vice; and then the great change comes. He is put in touch with a portion of the Great Memory, which Saint John has called the Book of Life. He becomes aware of all the emotions roused in his victims by his acts … No pain, no anguish he has caused has perished. All has been registered, has a kind of existence that makes him sensible of it once he has drifted into touch with the web of memory that clothed his life and the lives of those who came into contact with him on earth.

The history of the cruel man in the Hereafter would make a book which I am not permitted to write. I can only briefly add that his soul or mind becomes gradually purified through his identification with the sufferings of his victims.[239]

Decades later, the musician Donald Tovey made a similar claim through Rosemary Brown:

Each and every soul meets here with its just deserts, not because they are dispensed by a presiding deity, but because it is literally true that one reaps what one has sown. If one has endeavored to make the lot of others easier in earth-life and sought to promote the welfare and happiness of one's fellow-beings, then one finds oneself in a pleasing environment among congenial companions, and able to adapt without difficulty to the new mode of living. But those who have deliberately deprived others of their material rights and human needs, or have wantonly caused suffering, will find themselves in turn deprived and also imprisoned by their own meanness of outlook. This does not mean that they are trapped for ever in a self-made hell; the moment a soul sees and confesses its past misdeeds and attempts to rectify them, the way opens for it to evolve into the light.[240]

Julia, a communicator whom we will soon meet, echoed the messages received from Myers and Tovey:

Hell is on this side as well as Heaven. But it is the joy of Heaven to be always emptying Hell.[241]

---

239. Cummins, *The Road to Immortality*, 47.
240. Brown, *Immortals by My Side*, 105.
241. Stead, *Letters from Julia*, 25.

Ancient and Modern Revelation

Myers insists that there is no conflict between his words and those of the ancients.

> Apart from Revelations, what is the teaching of the Bible concerning the After-life? "We shall not all sleep, but we shall all be changed."
>
> The words of St. Paul harmonize with the account of the After-life given in these pages. The phrase "we shall not all sleep" implies that many do sleep until "the last trumpet sounds," until the end of the earth. In what garden, in what world, in what space to these sleepers rest?
>
> They are inhabitants of the world of illusion. Now, on that plane there is an almost entire absence of conflict and effort, accordingly there is an absence of any true creation. Many human beings regard such a state as the most desirable condition of being. Those of them who are satisfied with such a life meet it after death in the illusion world, and so linger within its borders until "the last trumpet sounds." This phrase of St. Paul's must be read symbolically. It possessed its own peculiar meaning in the ancient world, a meaning which has been lost. The souls who rest on the Third plane until they are roused by this summons may be fitly called "the sleepers." For what does sleep indicate if not an absence of conscious conflict and effort?
>
> Existence seems in many respects as real to the occupant of the world of illusion as it does to king, politician, lawyer, doctor, clergyman and working man on earth. But it contains one important difference. The soul has no need to put forth struggle or effort. He obtains his desire through the mere act of desire. So, he cannot be said to live as he did on earth, or gloriously as he will live in the world of Eidos. He is, in truth, the sleeper mentioned in the New Testament.

"We shall not all sleep, but we shall all be changed." This text infers that some of the dead do not sleep. In other words, many of those, who have died, scorn the pleasant fields of illusion; they desire conflict, creation, effort, and so they either become incarnate again or they wisely choose to go upwards and to enter the world of Eidos, to find life more abundantly within that masterpiece. For in that state, the traveler meets with the finest glories of appearance, with the triumph of life in form.[242]

On Reincarnation

The concept of the preexistence of the soul before birth had been widely held throughout the ancient world, not only among pagans, but also Jews and early Christians. As we have seen, nothing in the teachings of Jesus contradicts this idea; regardless, preexistence, and reincarnation along with it, was rejected by the Council of Constantinople in 553 AD (which, as mentioned earlier, Pope Vigilius did not call and refused to attend).

In his postmortem writings, Myers frequently mentions and praises Jesus, and occasionally mentions or quotes the apostles. He is also very clear that after and between each life on the plane of matter a period of time is spent on the third plane, described by Myers as "a resting place on the road." From the third plane humans and some of the higher animals may return again to Earth. Myers writes:

It must be remembered that we are not merely short stories on the pages of earth, we are a serial, and each chapter closes with a death. Yet the new chapter develops from those which preceded it, and we pick up the threads, continuing a narrative that has always design and purpose though the purpose may

242. Cummins, *The Road to Immortality*, 85–6.

be hidden because human beings, as a rule, are only permitted to study the one life, the one period of their history at a time.[243]

Regarding the number of times humans must again become incarnate, Myers adds:

I do not for a moment believe that the individual returns a hundred times or more to the earth. The majority of people only reincarnate two, three or four times. Though, if they have some human purpose or plan to achieve, they may return as many as eight or nine times. No arbitrary figure can be named. We are only safe in concluding that, in the human form, they are not doomed to wander over the space of fifty, a hundred and more lives.[244]

But Myers mentions a notable exception to these rules:

I am of the opinion that Christ was not an incarnation of Elisha or of any other human being. Christ was the limited expression of the Whole, the Word made flesh. He came but once to the earth and then returned to the Father. The long history of psychic evolution was not necessary to Christ.[245]

Love and Marriage

In common with other communicators, Myers also tells us that on the third plane we have a body that seems every bit as substantial as ours does now. Food and water are no longer required; sexual desires are in most cases still present, but women do not bear children. Regarding love and marriage, Myers writes:

243. Cummins, *Beyond Human Personality*, 25.
244. Cummins, *Beyond Human Personality*, 76.
245. Cummins, *Beyond Human Personality*, 81.

In the world after death men are the possessors of bodies which reproduce in shape and in general appearance the discarded physical form, though they are clothed in an ethereal substance.

Women do not bear children though sexual passion may be experienced as long as it is the soul's need. The woman possesses an etheric body so framed that it can serve her as the material shape served her various purposes, wishes, and appetites on earth.

The problem of marriage, of two husbands or of two wives, is usually solved after death by the pull of the stronger, finer affection. Each soul is either drawn to the one who is most akin and sympathetic to it, or is absorbed by whatever special passion or desire fills its nature.[246]

David Hatch, whom we will meet next, wrote:

There does seem to be a good deal of mating and rejoining of former mates. The sex distinction is as real here as on the earth, though, of course, its expression is not exactly the same.[247]

On Growth of the Spirit

Shortly after he died in 1912, Judge David Patterson Hatch began communicating frequently, until 1913, via automatic writing through his friend, the medium Elsa Barker, who compiled and published the series of messages in a beautiful book titled *Letters from the Light*. In these letters Hatch often mentions the wonderful opportunities for development available to all on the other side.

This is a great place in which to grow, if one really wants to grow; though few persons take advantage of its possibilities. There are teachers here who stand ready to help anyone who

246. Cummins, *Beyond Human Personality*, 36–7.
247. Barker, *Letters from the Light*, 55. "You are gods; you are all sons of the Most High," John 10:34.

wishes their help in making real and deep studies in the myster-
ies of life—the life here, the life there, and in the remote past.

If a man understands that his recent sojourn on earth was
merely the latest of a series of lives, and if he concentrates his
mind toward recovering the memories of the distant past, he
can recover them.[248]

In another letter delivered shortly afterward, Hatch elaborated
on how we are all capable of eventually becoming what men once
called gods.

I have had much joy in going back over my Greek incarna-
tions. What concentration they had—those Greeks! They knew
much. The waters of Lethe, for instance—what a concep-
tion!—brought from this side by masterly memory.

If man would even try to remember, if he would only take
time to consider all that he has been, there would be more
hope of what he may become! Why, do you know that man
may become a god—or that which, compared with ordinary
humanity, has all the magnitude and grandeur of a god? "Ye
are gods," was not said in a merely figurative sense.

I have met the Master of Galilee, and have held communion
with Him. There was a man—and a god! The world has need
of Him now.[249]

Art in the Next World

In one of the *Letters*, Hatch wrote:

I think the happiest people I have met on this side have been
the painters. Our matter is so light and subtle, and so easily
handled, that it falls readily into the forms of the imagination.
There are beautiful pictures here. Some of the artists try to

248. Barker, *Letters from the Light*, 57.
249. Barker, *Letters from the Light*, 100–101.

impress their pictures upon the mental eyes of the artists of the earth, and they often succeed in doing so.

There is joy in the heart of one of our real artists when a fellow craftsman on your side catches an idea from him and puts it into execution.

With poets it is the same. There are lovely lyrics composed out here and impressed upon the receptive minds of earthly poets.

It is much the same with musicians. Music on earth is much enjoyed on this side. Of all earthly things, sound reaches most directly into this plane of life. Tell that to the musicians.

If they could only hear our music! It seems sometimes as if you must hear our music over there, as we hear yours.[250]

Messages from other communicators are in agreement. The journalist, author, activist, and amateur medium William Thomas Stead calmly and courageously perished in 1912 with the sinking of *Titanic*, after being informed that the lifeboats were filled to capacity. However, in 1933 a book titled *Life Eternal* appeared, listing W. T. Stead as the author. In the introduction the medium Hester Dowden stated that it came to her via automatic writing from Stead. A brief excerpt:

The artists, including musicians and poets, are the happiest people who pass on to us. The sudden realization of clearer understanding of art and life is pure joy to them. They are our busiest people, and they radiate gladness. I must not forget to mention our actors, for theaters are as popular a form of art and amusement here as with you, and they, too, carry on their profession.

Music, however, has a wider field here than any of the other arts ... Everyone here is a musician to a certain degree. Almost

---

250. Barker, *Letters from the Light*, 49–51.

at once the need for music is felt, as hunger would be felt by you.[251]

Although music is described by some communicators as "the highest and most inspirational of the arts," "the supreme art," even "the veritable echoes of the majestic tones of the Almighty,"[252] it does not seem to be forced upon anyone who considers it a nuisance.

The air seems to be full of music. Not everybody has to pick it up, though. You only pick up the music if you want to. You don't need to have it if you don't want it. You can shut it out and be in silence.

And from the son of Sir Oliver Lodge:

There are places on my sphere where they can listen to beautiful music when they choose. Everybody, even here, doesn't care for music, so it's not in my sphere compulsory.[253]

Science in the Next World

Those individuals interested in scientific pursuits also have free rein and ample resources. From three different sources:

Our scientific researches and investigations are extended to all that pertains to the phenomena of universal nature; to all the wonders of the heavens and the Earth, and to whatever the mind of man is capable of conceiving: all of which exercises our faculties, and form a considerable part of our enjoyments.

I am studying science, which I always liked—really and actually the science of life, the cause of things—and something of

251. Stead, *Life Eternal*, 102.
252. All three quoted in Porteous, *Spiritual Reality and the Afterlife*, 360.
253. Both quoted in Allen, *The Realities of Heaven*, 163.

the marvelous universe and of the natural laws which govern everything.

The noble and sublime sciences of astronomy, chemistry, and mathematics, engage a considerable portion of our attention, and afford us an inexhaustible subject for study and reflection.[254]

A Promise Kept

William Stead, whom we met earlier, had known a woman named Julia, who had made a solemn covenant with her good friend Ellen that whoever would be taken first would, if possible, return and make her presence known.

Julia died first, in her youth, in the United States in 1891. Stead wrote:

> One night the promise was fulfilled. Ellen was sleeping in her old home, when suddenly she was waked up. It was night, but the room was full of light. And close to her bedside she saw Julia in her habit as she lived, radiant with life and peace and joy. She had redeemed her promise. For some moments she stood there, smiling but silent. Ellen was too awestruck to speak. The sudden and unmistakable fulfillment of the desire of her heart seemed to rob her of all her faculty but that of feeling unspeakable joy. Then the figure slowly, almost imperceptibly, dissolved away, and Ellen was once more alone.[255]

Several months later Julia appeared again to Ellen, this time in a country house in England in which Stead was also staying. Since Julia had been a mutual friend, Ellen told Stead the story of the two visits. Stead had recently discovered, to his surprise, that he had the ability of an automatic writing medium, and suggested that Julia be allowed to write through his hand. The resulting

---

254. All three quoted in Allen, *The Realities of Heaven*, 156.
255. Stead, *Letters from Julia*, 12–13.

communications took the form of letters, first to Ellen, then to Stead, and were written during 1892 to1897. Stead then published the collection as *Letters from Julia*.

Since Julia had passed over in 1891, many of the early letters deal with her early experiences on the other side. After a few years, the letters began to deal with other topics. In March of 1895 the following was received through Stead's hand.

The Meeting with Jesus

When I had tried in vain to communicate with Minerva and with Ellen, I began to be a little sad. It seemed to me as if I were away from the real interests which bound me to life. Then it was that the Good Angel who had welcomed me into this world took me to see my Lord.

It was beautiful and glorious, exceeding all my powers of description. There was no expectation of the meeting; nor was I even able to realize the fact that I had met Him until I saw the whole landscape flame and glow as with the radiance of opened heaven when He spoke to me. The cause for this diffi-culty was, I suppose, the extreme naturalness of all that I saw and heard. When there is something of what we used to call the supernatural order coming in the midst of what seems so very natural, it is difficult to realize it. But, oh, my friend, when it is realized, what a change occurs! The whole world was transfigured in the realization of the intensity and constancy of His love. And from that moment I have never been sad, save for my own short-comings and my own lack of love. Oh, my dearest friend, if only we could live more in the realized sense of His love.[256]

Stead then asked: "What about the divinity of our Lord?" Julia replied:

---

256. Stead, *Letters from Julia*, 68–9.

Why do you trouble yourselves about these scholasticisms? The thing that matters to you is surely what is—not what may have been defined centuries since. When you come to this side and have a more vivid sense of the majesty and marvel of the universe, then you see, as we do every day, the great unfolding of the infinite glory of the Infinite Father; and when you see also, as we do, that the whole secret of all things is Love, and that here was never so much Love revealed to mankind as in Him, you can understand how it is true that there dwelt in Him the fullness of the God-head bodily.[257]

This rejection of arcane theological dogma is echoed in the communications of a being who called himself Imperator, chief control of William Stanton Moses, ordained clergyman of the Church of England, who first scorned and denounced mediumship, and then was later was surprised to discover that he himself was a gifted medium. Moses sometimes had difficulty reconciling the detailed messages that were delivered via his own automatic writing with his very conventional Anglican beliefs. For instance:

Religion is not so abstruse a problem as man has made it. The theological speculations, the dogmatic definitions with which man has overlaid the revelation of God, serve but to perplex and bewilder, and to involve the spirit struggling up to light in the mists and fogs of ignorance and superstition.[258]

• • •

A central theme of many messages is the importance of being conscious of the responsibility of our earthly lives. From Stead's friend Julia:

---

257. Stead, *Letters from Julia*, 69.
258. As quoted in Porteous, *Spiritual Reality and the Afterlife*, 380.

You may think it strange that the verification of another life should increase the importance of this. But such is the fact, and you can never understand the importance of your life until you see it from this side. You are never, for one moment, idle from influencing eternity.[259]

In December of 1922 Arthur Conan Doyle began receiving messages from a being that identified himself as Pheneas, and who claimed to have died thousands of years earlier. Perhaps this passage best sums up the essence of the most advanced communications:

Love, not fear, must reign in each heart. Humanity must know the kind of existence they will lead in the lower greyer spheres if their lives are selfish and evil in the earth plane. Knowledge of where a man's actions are leading him will help and inspire him to live at his highest and what to avoid. The knowledge of the real and human happiness in the higher worlds ahead will give a man courage in facing sorrows and difficulties on this earth. The hope and joy of great happiness and the fulfillment of all his heart's ideals will make life here so much easier to bear, and so much more radiant.[260]

When we are born, we cry, and our families rejoice.
When we die, our families cry, and we rejoice.
—Tibetan folk saying

---

259. Stead, *Letters from Julia*, 95.
260. As quoted in Tymn, *The Afterlife Revealed*, 159.

Bibliography

Allen, Miles Edward. *The Realities of Heaven: Fifty Spirits Describe Your Future Home*. Momentum Media, CreateSpace Independent Publishing Platform, 2015.

Almeder, Robert. *Death and Personal Survival*. Rowman and Littlefield, 1992.

Anderson, E. W. "Abnormal Mental States in Survivors, with Special Reference to Collective Hallucinations." *Royal Naval Medical Service Journal* 28 (1942): 361–377.

Austen, A. W., ed. *Teachings of Silver Birch*. Spiritual Truth Foundation, 1938.

Barker, Elsa. *Letters from the Light: An Afterlife Journal*. Beyond Words Publishing, 1995.

Barrett, William. *Death Bed Visions*. Methuen, 1926.

Bayfield, M. A. "Notes on the Same Scripts." *Proceedings of the Society for Psychical Research* XXVII (1914–1915): 244–49.

Beloff, John. "The Mind-Brain Problem." *The Journal of Scientific Exploration* 8, no. 4 (1994): 509–22.

Boycott, B. B. "Learning in the Octopus." *Scientific American* 212 (1965): 42–50.

Braude, S. "Evaluating the Super-psi Hypothesis." In *Exploring the Paranormal: Perspectives on Belief and Experience*. Edited by George Zollschan, John Schumaker, and Greg Walsh. Prism Press, 1989.

———. *Immortal Remains*. Rowman and Littlefield, 2003.

———. *The Limits of Influence*. Routledge, 1991.

Broad, CD. *Lectures on Psychical Research*. Humanities Press, 1962.

———. *The Mind and Its Place in Nature*. Harcourt, Brace and Company, 1929.

Broome, K., producer. *The Day I Died: The Mind, the Brain, and Near-Death Experiences*. Motion picture. Films for the Humanities and Sciences, 2002.

Broughton, Richard, and Cheryl Alexander. "Autoganzfeld II: The First 100 Sessions." *Proceedings of the 38th Annual Parapsychological Association Convention* (1997): 53–61.

Brown, Rosemary. *Immortals by My Side*. Bachman and Turner, 1974.

Burt, Cyril. *ESP and Psychology*. Edited by Anita Gregory. Weidenfeld and Nicolson, 1975.

Carter, Chris. "Response to 'Could Pam Reynolds Hear?'" *Journal of Near-Death Studies* 30, no. 1 (Fall 2011): 29–53.

———. *Science and the Afterlife*. Inner Traditions, 2012.

———. *Science and the Near-Death Experience*. Inner Traditions, 2010.

———. *Science and Psychic Phenomena: The Fall of the House of Skeptics*. Inner Traditions, 2012.

Clarke, Arthur C. "World of Strange Powers: Messages from the Dead." Yorkshire Television. Available on Pacific Arts Video, 1985.

Colvin, Geoff. *Talent is Overrated*. Penguin Books, 2008.

Cousins, W. E. "Writer, Medium, Suffragette, Spy? The Unseen Adventures of Geraldine Cummins." *Paranormal Review* 45 (2008): 3–7.

Crookall, Robert. *The Supreme Adventure: Analysis of Psychic Communications*. James Clarke and Co., 1961.

Crossley, Alan. *The Story of Helen Duncan*. Psychic World Publications, 1975.

Cummins, Geraldine. *Beyond Human Personality*. Psychic Press, 1935.

———. *The Road to Immortality*. 4th ed. Lowe and Brydone, 1932, 1967.

———, and Signe Toksvig. *Swan on a Black Sea*. Routledge and Kegan Paul, 1965.

Currie, Ian. *You Cannot Die!* Somerville House, 1978.

Dennett, D. C. *Consciousness Explained*. Little Brown, 1991.

Ducasse, Curt. *Paranormal Science and Life After Death*. Charles C. Thomas, 1959.

———. "What Would Constitute Conclusive Evidence of Survival after Death?" *Journal of the Society for Psychical Research* 41, no. 714 (1962): 401–6.

Edmonds, John Edwards. *Letters and Tracts on Spiritualism*. J. Burns Progressive Library, 1874.

———. *Spiritualism: Volume 2*. J. Partridge and Brittan, 1855.

Eisenbeiss, W., and D. Hassler. "An Assessment of Ostensible Communications with a Deceased Grandmaster as Evidence for Survival." *Journal of the Society for Psychical Research* 70.2, no. 883 (April 2006): 65–97.

Fenwick, Peter, and Elizabeth Fenwick. *The Truth in the Light*. London: Headline Book Publishing, 1995.

Gauld, Alan. "Discarnate Survival." *Handbook of Parapsychology*. Edited by B. Wolman. Van Nostrand Reinhold, 1977.

———. *Mediumship and Survival: A Century of Investigations*. William Heinemann, 1982.

Gordon, Henry. *Extrasensory Deception*. Toronto: Macmillan of Canada, 1988.

Griffen, DR. *Parapsychology, Philosophy, and Spirituality*. SUNY Press, 1997.

Lieut. A. M. H. "An Apparition Identified from a Photograph." *Journal of the American Society for Psychical Research* 20 (1931): 53–57.

Hameroff, S. "Response to 'Could Pam Reynolds Hear?'" *Journal of Near-Death Studies* 30, no. 1 (Fall 2011): 26–28.

Hamilton, Margaret Lillian. *Is Survival a Fact? Studies of Deep-Trance Automatic Scripts and the Bearing of Intentional Actions by the Trance Personalities on the Question of Human Survival*. Psychic Press, 1969.

Hamrick, Cliff. "Book Review: Science and the Afterlife Experience." *Journal of Near-Death Studies* 31, no. 1 (Fall 2012): 30–33.

Hansel, C. E. M. *ESP and Parapsychology: A Critical Re-Evaluation*. Prometheus, 1966, 1980.

Haraldsson, E. "Survey of Claimed Encounters with the Dead." *Omega* 19, no. 2 (1988): 103–113.

Hart, Hornell. *The Enigma of Survival: The Case For and Against the After Life*. Rider, 1959.

Herbert, N. *Elemental Mind: Human Consciousness and the New Physics*. Penguin Books, 1993.

Heywood, Rosalind. *Beyond the Reach of Sense*. E. P. Dutton & Company, 1961.

Hodgson, R. "A Further Record of Observations of Certain Phenomena of Trance." *Proceedings of the Society for Psychical Research* 13 (1897): 284–582.

Horgan, Craig. *Your Eternal Self*. Greater Reality Publications, 2008.

Hyslop, J. H. *Life After Death*. Kessinger Publishing, 1918.

Inglis, Brian. *Natural and Supernatural*. Hodder and Stoughton, 1977.

James, William. *The Will to Believe, Human Immortality, and Other Essays on Popular Philosophy*. New York: Dover, 1956. Original works published 1897, 1898.

Kelly, Edward, et al. *Irreducible Mind*. Rowman and Littlefield, 2009.

Lennox, John. *God's Undertaker? Has Science Buried God?* Lion Hudson, 2009.

Lieut. A. M. H. "An Apparition Identified from a Photograph." *Journal of the American Society for Psychical Research* 20 (1931): 53–57.

Lodge, Oliver. "Evidence of Classical Scholarship and of Cross-Correspondence in Some New Automatic Writings." *Proceedings of the Society for Psychical Research*, part LXIII (June 1911): 113–75.

Lomaxe, Paul. "Judge Edmonds: A Psychic Sensitive." General Assembly of Spiritualists, 1945.

Lorimer, David. *Survival? Body, Mind and Death in the Light of Psychic Experience*. Routledge and Kegan Paul, 1984.

May EC, Marwaha SB. "An alternative hypothesis for the Géza Maróczy (via medium Rollans) vs. Viktor Korchnoi chess game." *Academia* 116 (2021). https://www.academia.edu/31084244.

McGrew, Timothy. "The Simulation of Expertise: Deeper Blue and the Riddle of Cognition," Origins and Design 19.1 (1998). Accessed March 15 2012 from http://www.arn.org/docs/odesign/od191/deeperblue191.htm

Moody, Raymond. *Life After Life*. New York: Mockingbird Books, 1975.

Morton, R. C. "Record of a Haunted House." *Proceedings of the Society for Psychical Research* III (1892): 311–332.

Myers, Frederic. "On Recognized Apparitions Occurring More Than a Year after Death." *Proceedings of the Society for Psychical Research* 6 (1889–90): 13–65.

Nahm, M. "Terminal Lucidity in People with Mental Illness and Other Mental Disability." *Journal of Near-Death Studies* 28, no. 2 (Winter 2009): 86–106.

———, and B. Greyson. "Terminal Lucidity in Patients with Chronic Schizophrenia and Dementia." *Journal of Nervous and Mental Disease* 197, no. 12 (December 2009): 942–944.

———, B. Greyson, E. W. Kelly, and E. Haraldsson. "Terminal Lucidity: A Review and a Case Collection." *Archives of Gerontology and Geriatrics* 58 (2011): 138–142.

Nash, Michael. "The Truth and the Hype of Hypnosis." *Scientific American* (2001). https://www.ocf.berkeley.edu/~jfkihlstrom/ConsciousnessWeb/PDFs/SciAm0701.pdf.

Neppe, Vernon. "A Detailed Analysis of an Important Chess Game: Revisiting 'Maroczy versus Korchnoi.'" *Journal of the Society for Psychical Research* 71.3, no. 888 (July 2007): 129–47.

Osis, K., and E. Haraldsson. *At the Hour of Death*. Avon Books, 1977.

Piddington, J. G. "A Series of Concordant Automisms." *Proceedings of the Society for Psychical Research* 22 (1908): 86–169.

———. "Three Incidents from the Sitting: Lethe, the Sibyl, the Horace Ode Question." *Proceedings of the Society for Psychical Research* 24 (1910): 86–169.

Popper, Karl. "Replies to my Critics." In *The Philosophy of Karl Popper*, part II. Edited by Paul Arthur Shilpp. The Open Court Publishing Company, 1974.

Porteous, D. C. *Spiritual Reality and the Afterlife*. Hawkshaw House, 2022.

Potts, Michael, and Amy Devanno. "Tertullian's Theory of the Soul." *Journal of the Society for Psychical Research* 77, no. 913 (October 2013): 213.

Rao, K. Ramakrishna. "Consciousness." In *Encyclopedia of Psychology* 1, 2nd ed. Edited by Raymond Corsini. John Wiley and Sons, 1994.

Ring, Kenneth, and Sharon Cooper. *Mindsight*. William James Center for Consciousness Studies, 1999.

Rivas, T., A. Dirven, and R. Smit. *The Self Does Not Die*. 2nd ed. International Association for Near-Death Studies, 2023.

Rosenblum, B., and F. Kuttner. "Consciousness and Quantum Mechanics: The Connection and Analogies." *The Journal of Mind and Behaviour* 20, no. 3 (Summer 1999): 229–56.

Rudy, Dr. Lloyd. "Dr. Lloyd Rudy, Famous Cardiac Surgeon, Talks about the Importance of Oral Systemic Health [2-Part Interview]." *American Academy for Oral Systemic Health* (2011, June 24–25). Retrieved from http:// oralsystemiclink.pro/heart -attack-stroke/1st-scientific-session-of-the-academy-for-oral -systemichealth/.

Russell, Bertrand. *A History of Western Philosophy*. George Allen and Unwin, 1946.

Sabom, M. *Light and Death*. Zondervan, 1998.

Saltmarsh, Herbert. *Evidence of Personal Survival from Cross Correspondences*. G. Bell and Sons, 1938.

Sheldrake, Rupert. "Can Our Memories Survive the Death of Our Brains?" In *What Survives?* Edited by Gary Doore. Jeremy P. Tarcher, 1990.

———. *The Rebirth of Nature*. Bantam Books, 1991.

———. *The Science Delusion*. Coronet, 2012.

———. *The Sense of Being Stared At, And Other Aspects of the Extended Mind*. Hutchinson, 2003.

Sherwood, Jane. *The Country Beyond*. Neville Spearman, 1969. First edition, 1944.

Stapp, H. *Mindful Universe*. Springer, 2007.

Stead, W. T. *Letters from Julia*. White Crow, 2011.

———. *Life Eternal*. Wright and Brown, 1933.

Stevenson, Ian. *Cases of the Reincarnation Type: Volume 1, Ten Cases in India*. University Press of Virginia, 1975.

———. *Children Who Remember Previous Lives*. University Press of Virginia, 1987.

———. "The Contribution of Apparitions to the Evidence for Survival." *Journal of the Society for Psychical Research* 76 (1982): 341–58.

Targ, Russel. *Do You See What I See?* Hampton Roads Publishing Company, 2008.

Thomas, Drayton. "A New Hypothesis Concerning Trance Communications." *Proceedings of the Society for Psychical Research* XLVIII, part 173 (1949): 121–63.

———. "A Proxy Extending Over Eleven Sittings with Mrs. Osborne Leonard." Proceedings of the Society for Psychical Research XLIII, part 142 (1935): 439–519.

Tweedale, Charles. *Man's Survival After Death*. Psychic Book Club, 1909.

Tymn, Michael. *The Afterlife Revealed: What Happens After We Die*. White Crow Books, 2011.

———. "Bible Scholar Explores Modern Psychic Phenomena." Posted online January 2, 2023, at http://whitecrowbooks.com /michaeltymn/.

Utts, J. M. "An Assessment of the Evidence for Psychic Functioning." *Journal of Scientific Exploration* 10, no. 1 (1996): 3–30.

Walker, E. H. "The Nature of Consciousness." *Mathematical Biosciences* 7 (1970): 131.

William, James. *The Will to Believe, Human Immortality, and other Essays*. Dover, 1956. Original works published 1897, 1898.

Woerlee, G. "Could Pam Reynolds Hear?" *Journal of Near-Death Studies* 30, no. 1 (Fall 2011): 3–25.

Yuille, J., and J. Cutshall. "A Case Study of Eyewitness Memory to a Crime." *Journal of Applied Psychology* 71, no. 2 (1986): 291–301.

To Write to the Author

If you wish to contact the author or would like more information about this book, please write to the author in care of Llewellyn Worldwide Ltd. and we will forward your request. Both the author and the publisher appreciate hearing from you and learning of your enjoyment of this book and how it has helped you. Llewellyn Worldwide Ltd. cannot guarantee that every letter written to the author can be answered, but all will be forwarded. Please write to:

Chris Carter
⅍ Llewellyn Worldwide
2143 Wooddale Drive
Woodbury, MN 55125-2989

Please enclose a self-addressed stamped envelope for reply,
or $1.00 to cover costs. If outside the U.S.A., enclose
an international postal reply coupon.

Many of Llewellyn's authors have websites with additional information and resources. For more information, please visit our website at http://www.llewellyn.com.